Divorce *in Nevada*

The Legal Process,
Your Rights, and What to Expect

Marshal S. Willick, Esq.

Addicus Books
Omaha, Nebraska

An Addicus Nonfiction Book

ISBN 978-1-938803-64-2

Typography Jack Kusler

This book is not intended to serve as a substitute for an attorney. Nor is it the author's intent to give legal advice contrary to that of an attorney. The information contained in this book is for general informational purposes only and should not be relied upon or considered legal advice applicable to a specific legal matter.

Library of Congress Cataloging-in-Publication Data

Willick, Marshal, 1958- author.

Divorce in Nevada : the legal process, your rights, and what to expect / Marshal Willick.

pages cm — (Divorce in)

Includes bibliographical references and index.

ISBN 978-1-938803-64-2 (paperback)

1. Divorce—Nevada—Popular works. I. Title.

KFN700.W55 2014

346.79301'66—dc23

2014010587

Addicus Books, Inc.
P.O. Box 45327
Omaha, Nebraska 68145
www.AddicusBooks.com

Printed in the United States of America

10 9 8 7 6 5 4 3 2 1

To Jerry and Birdie Willick, who taught by example, quiet courage, endurance, and selfless service, and who gave me the opportunity to become whatever I chose to be.

Contents

Foreword

After having worked in the family law arena as an attorney for two decades, and now interpreting those laws from the bench, I believe I have a good understanding of the interplay between the "law" and the "family." Although "family law" covers relatively few sections of the Nevada Revised Statutes and some Supreme Court decisions, its perceived simplicity ends there. The actual process from start to finish is daunting.

As family division judges, we are committed to providing families and children with safe, fair, courteous, and efficient dispute resolution and justice, but we can only act upon the information provided to us.

In family court, judges make decisions, that affect families not only now, but also, in many instances, for decades into the future. An understanding of how to effectively present your case is vital to obtaining a decision that appropriately applies the existing law to your specific facts.

Obtaining that information can only be considered a positive step in this process. It is my hope that the information in this book is helpful to divorcing individuals in successfully navigating the family court system.

Honorable Charles J. Hoskin
Presiding Judge, Family Division
Eighth Judicial District Court

Acknowledgments

This book owes its existence to a lot of folks, in a lot of ways. I owe much to the attorneys and staff of the Willick Law Group, who keep the place operating while I engage in such projects, especially Faith Fish, who somehow makes sure all the checks clear, and Richard Crane, who did the heavy lifting of putting the pieces together to make this book project do-able.

My thanks to Jennifer Abrams, an experienced, talented, and wise matrimonial lawyer in her own right, for both proofreading and reality-checking. Thanks to Sarah Willick for not being afraid to tell her old man about the misuse of commas. And I owe a debt to the memory of my brother Seth, whose disapproving glare and implied "Keep it simple, stupid!" I saw and heard every time a four-syllable word appeared in the text where a one-syllable one would do.

I thank all my clients, past and present, whose questions made their way into this book. And finally, thanks to Rod Colvin, my publisher, and his team from Addicus Books, for their patience during the drafting of this book.

Introduction

Divorce can be a scary process. It is almost always emotionally and financially challenging. There has long been a need for a reference, written in plain English, from which ordinary men and women can get answers about how the divorce process works in Nevada and what to expect. This book is my attempt to meet that need. It is my hope that it makes a difficult time in the life of its readers less intimidating and thus more bearable.

Like any handbook, this one is no substitute for the advice of an attorney. It is intended only to give you some idea of what is involved in the divorce process and to help you and your lawyer work together more effectively.

Mainly, this book addresses common issues in the legal aspects of divorce in general terms, but some attention is also given to the emotional aspects. The hope is that it will provide some assistance when you have to make rational decisions likely to affect you and your children for a very long time, just when you are feeling most upset and it is difficult to be logical.

Most decisions made entirely from emotion are poor ones. Wherever possible, stay calm, and try to do those things that—ten or twenty years from now—you'll wish you had done. Seeing the long view will go far in helping you stay focused on making the decisions most likely to benefit you. It has been said that "there are no winners in divorce litigation—only survivors." It is our hope that this book contributes to the successful completion of this journey with as little damage as possible, and with the greatest possible likelihood of an improved future.

bout protecting yourself and your children. No legitimate awyer will encourage you to proceed with a divorce unless ou have decided that is the only option for you.

Ask what documents you should bring to your initial onsultation. Make a list of your questions to bring to that first neeting. Start making plans for how you will pay your attorney o begin work on your case, and make sure you can afford the ttorney that you hire. Having all of the information necessary o move forward intelligently is extremely important.

Not all attorneys are alike. If you have a fairly simple ase—short-duration marriage, no children, and few assets and lebts—any family law attorney should be able to assist you. However, if you have complex or emotionally charged issues, you should consider seeking representation from a lawyer with credentials indicating a higher level of specialized training and expertise.

In Nevada, this would mean a *family law specialist,* or a member of the American Academy of Matrimonial Lawyers (AAML). The state bar keeps a list of certified specialists at http://www.nvbar.org/content/certified-specialists. You can find a list of AAML members at www.AAML.org.

1.2 Must I have an attorney to get a divorce in Nevada?

No. You are not required to have an attorney to obtain a divorce in Nevada. However, if your case involves children, alimony, significant property, debts, or other complex issues, you should seriously consider hiring counsel. Remember the adage attributed to Abe Lincoln: “A man who represents himself has a fool for a client.”

If you choose to represent yourself, you will be expected to follow all rules and procedures as if you were an attorney. Failure to do things properly or adequately to protect your own rights may result in irreversible negative consequences. In other words, if you make mistakes while acting on your own behalf, it may be impossible for any lawyer to fix those mistakes.

If you are convinced that you can or are determined to represent yourself, you can find forms intended to assist you at either the self help center located at the Family Court website or on our website at www.willicklawgroup.com.

1

Understanding the Divorce Pro

At a time when your life can feel like it's in utt sometimes the smallest bit of predictability c a sense of comfort. The outcome of many aspects divorce may be unknown, increasing your fear and But there is one part of your divorce that does ha measure of predictability, and that is the divorce proce

Most divorces proceed in a step-by-step manner. the uniqueness of your divorce, you can generally c one phase of your divorce following the next. Someti realizing you are completing stages and moving forw your divorce can reassure you that it won't go on fore

Develop a basic understanding of the divorce This will lower your anxiety when your attorney starts about "depositions" or "going to trial," and you feel yo start pounding in fear. It can reduce your frustration ab length of the process because you understand why each needed. It will support you to begin preparing for what next.

Most importantly, understanding the divorce p will make your experience of the entire divorce easie wouldn't prefer that?

1.1 What is my first step?

Find a law firm that handles divorces as a regular p its law practice. The best recommendations come from p who have knowledge of a lawyer's experience and reput

If you are considering divorce but are not ready to fil an attorney to schedule an appointment to obtain inform

1

Understanding the Divorce Process

At a time when your life can feel like it's in utter chaos, sometimes the smallest bit of predictability can bring a sense of comfort. The outcome of many aspects of your divorce may be unknown, increasing your fear and anxiety. But there is one part of your divorce that does have some measure of predictability, and that is the divorce process itself.

Most divorces proceed in a step-by-step manner. Despite the uniqueness of your divorce, you can generally count on one phase of your divorce following the next. Sometimes just realizing you are completing stages and moving forward with your divorce can reassure you that it won't go on forever.

Develop a basic understanding of the divorce process. This will lower your anxiety when your attorney starts talking about "depositions" or "going to trial," and you feel your heart start pounding in fear. It can reduce your frustration about the length of the process because you understand why each step is needed. It will support you to begin preparing for what comes next.

Most importantly, understanding the divorce process will make your experience of the entire divorce easier. Who wouldn't prefer that?

1.1 What is my first step?

Find a law firm that handles divorces as a regular part of its law practice. The best recommendations come from people who have knowledge of a lawyer's experience and reputation.

If you are considering divorce but are not ready to file, call an attorney to schedule an appointment to obtain information about protecting yourself and your children. No legitimate lawyer will encourage you to proceed with a divorce unless you have decided that is the only option for you.

Ask what documents you should bring to your initial consultation. Make a list of your questions to bring to that first meeting. Start making plans for how you will pay your attorney to begin work on your case, and make sure you can afford the attorney that you hire. Having all of the information necessary to move forward intelligently is extremely important.

Not all attorneys are alike. If you have a fairly simple case—short-duration marriage, no children, and few assets and debts—any family law attorney should be able to assist you. However, if you have complex or emotionally charged issues, you should consider seeking representation from a lawyer with credentials indicating a higher level of specialized training and expertise.

In Nevada, this would mean a *family law specialist,* or a member of the American Academy of Matrimonial Lawyers (AAML). The state bar keeps a list of certified specialists at http://www.nvbar.org/content/certified-specialists. You can find a list of AAML members at www.AAML.org.

1.2 Must I have an attorney to get a divorce in Nevada?

No. You are not required to have an attorney to obtain a divorce in Nevada. However, if your case involves children, alimony, significant property, debts, or other complex issues, you should seriously consider hiring counsel. Remember the adage attributed to Abe Lincoln: "A man who represents himself has a fool for a client."

If you choose to represent yourself, you will be expected to follow all rules and procedures as if you were an attorney. Failure to do things properly or adequately to protect your own rights may result in irreversible negative consequences. In other words, if you make mistakes while acting on your own behalf, it may be impossible for any lawyer to fix those mistakes.

If you are convinced that you can or are determined to represent yourself, you can find forms intended to assist you at either the self help center located at the Family Court website or on our website at www.willicklawgroup.com.

A person who proceeds in a legal matter without a lawyer is referred to as being *pro se* (pronounced "pro say"), meaning on one's own. You will also hear it referred to as "appearing in proper person."

If you are considering proceeding without an attorney, at a minimum have an initial consultation with an attorney to discuss your rights and duties under the law. You may have rights or obligations you don't even know exist. Meeting with a lawyer can help you decide whether to proceed on your own.

1.3 What steps are taken during the divorce process?

The divorce process in Nevada typically involves the steps listed below.

- Obtain a referral for a lawyer.
- Schedule an appointment with an attorney.
- Prepare questions and gather needed documents for the initial consultation.
- Meet for the initial consultation with attorney.
- Pay retainer to attorney and sign retainer agreement.
- Provide requested information and documents to attorney.
- Take preliminary actions as advised by attorney, such as opening or closing financial accounts.
- Attorney prepares complaint for divorce, summons, and preliminary injunction for your review and signature.
- Attorney files complaint with the court, has the summons issued, and issues the injunction.
- Spouse is served with all filed documents by a process server.
- Negotiations begin regarding terms of temporary orders on matters such as custody, support, and temporary possession of the family home. Attorneys prepare financial disclosure forms and child-support guidelines for temporary hearing.
- Case management conference/temporary order hearing is held.

OR

- Parties reach agreement on temporary orders.
- Trial date and discovery deadlines are set.
- Temporary orders are prepared by one attorney, approved as to form and content by the other attorney, and submitted to the judge for signature.
- If there are minor children, parties comply with any local rules or court orders to attend parent education class, develop a parenting plan, or participate in mediation.
- Both sides conduct discovery to obtain information regarding all relevant facts. Obtain valuations of all assets, including expert opinions if needed.
- Confer with attorney to review facts, identify issues, assess strengths and weaknesses of you case, review strategy, and develop proposal for settlement.
- Spouses, with the support of their attorneys, attempt to reach agreement through written proposals, mediation, settlement conferences, or other negotiation.
- Parties reach agreement on all issues.

OR

- Parties prepare for trial on unresolved issues.
- Preparations proceed and include the preparation of witnesses, trial exhibits, legal research on contested issues, pretrial motions, trial brief, preparation of direct and cross-examination of witnesses, preparation of opening statement, subpoena of witnesses, and closing argument and suggestions to the court.
- Attorney prepares decree and court orders for the division of retirement plans for approval by spouses and attorneys.
- Meet with attorney for final trial preparation.
- Trial is held.
- Judge makes decision.
- Attorney prepares decree. Spouse's attorney approves decree as to form.

- Decree submitted to judge for signature.
- Judge signs decree of divorce. Make payments and sign documents (deeds or titles) according to decree.

1.4 Is Nevada a *no-fault* state or do I need grounds for a divorce?

Nevada, like most states, is a "no-fault" divorce state. This means that neither you nor your spouse is required to prove that the other is "at fault" in order to be granted a divorce. It is not necessary to allege or prove factors such as infidelity, cruelty, or abandonment to receive a divorce in Nevada. Rather, the only required assertions are "incompatibility" (that you and your spouse can no longer live as husband and wife) and that there is no chance of reconciliation.

Older grounds for divorce (insanity existing for two years before filing, or separation for more than one year) are still "on the books" but are essentially never used.

The only "proof" of incompatibility usually required is testimony by either you or your spouse, which is likely to be sufficient evidence for the court to rule that the marriage should be dissolved.

Many divorces are granted "on the papers" without a court appearance. If there is a "prove up" hearing, however, this testimony must be given, usually by the spouse who filed the initial complaint for divorce. He or she will be asked (or "canvassed") those simple questions.

Don't be surprised by the lack of interest by the judge in any "reasons" why the marriage failed. It is simply irrelevant to whether a divorce will be granted.

1.5 Do I have to get divorced in the same state I married in?

No. Regardless of where you were married, you may seek a divorce in Nevada if the jurisdictional requirements of residency are met.

1.6 How long must I have lived in Nevada to get a divorce in the state?

Either you or your spouse must have been a resident of Nevada for at least six weeks before the complaint for divorce is filed. This residency requirement is very short compared to most states and makes Nevada a popular place for parties to come to seek a divorce.

The judge will need "corroboration" that one of the parties is a Nevada resident. Usually, this is provided by testimony or a short affidavit of a resident witness who may have to testify that either you or your spouse was a resident (i.e., that the witness has seen you physically present in Nevada) for at least six weeks before the complaint was filed.

1.7 My spouse has told me that she will never "give" me a divorce. Can I get one in Nevada anyway?

Yes. Nevada does not require that your spouse agree to a divorce. If your spouse threatens to not "give" you a divorce, know that in Nevada this is likely to be an idle threat without any basis. Under Nevada law, to obtain a divorce you must only show that the court has jurisdiction over one of the parties to the marriage to affect the "status" (i.e., make you single instead of married).

In short, it is not necessary to have your spouse agree to the divorce or to allege the specific difficulties that arose during the marriage to obtain a divorce in Nevada.

1.8 Can I divorce my spouse in Nevada if he or she lives in another state?

Yes. Provided you have met the residency requirements for living in Nevada for six weeks, you can file for divorce here even if your spouse lives in another state.

Discuss with your attorney the facts of your case, the steps necessary to give your spouse proper notice, and whether the court will have jurisdiction over your spouse and all the "incidents" of your marriage. Those are the subjects that come up in divorce, such as division of property, child custody, and spousal support. It is possible that a Nevada divorce court might have jurisdiction to grant the divorce, but not to affect property or require the payment of money from one party to another.

Your attorney can counsel you on whether it is possible to proceed with the divorce and warn you of the pitfalls of proceeding without proper jurisdiction over your spouse.

1.9 How can I divorce my spouse when I don't know where my spouse lives now?

Nevada law allows you to proceed with a divorce even if you do not know the current address of your spouse.

First, take action to attempt to locate your spouse. Contact family members, friends, former coworkers, or anyone else who might know your spouse's whereabouts. Utilize resources on the Internet that are designed to help locate people. This is known as "doing your due diligence."

Let your attorney know of the efforts you have made to attempt to find your spouse. Inform your lawyer of your spouse's last known address, as well as any work address or other address where he or she may be found. If your attorney attempts to give notice to your spouse under the procedural rules without success, it is possible to ask the court to proceed with the divorce by giving notice through publication in a newspaper, although this extends the time to finish the divorce by a few weeks.

While your divorce may be granted following service of notice by publication in a newspaper, you may not have jurisdiction over valuable assets such as pension plans unless it can be shown to the court that the "last matrimonial domicile" (where you last lived as husband and wife) was in Nevada. Talk to your attorney about your options and rights if you don't know where your spouse is living.

1.10 I just moved to a different county within the state of Nevada. Do I have to file in the county where my spouse lives?

You may file your divorce complaint either in the county where you reside or in the county where your spouse resides. But the case might be moved to the county where the defendant lives.

1.11 I immigrated to Nevada. Will my immigration status stop me from getting a divorce?

No. If you meet the residency requirements for divorce in Nevada, you can get a divorce here notwithstanding your immigration status.

If you are a woman and a victim of domestic violence, tell your lawyer. You may be eligible for a change in your immigration status under the federal *Violence Against Women Act* or other laws.

1.12 I want to get divorced in my Indian tribal court. What do I need to know?

Each tribal court has its own laws governing divorce. Requirements for residency, grounds for divorce, and the laws regarding property, alimony, and children can vary substantially from state law. Some tribes have very different laws governing the grounds for your divorce, removal of children from the home, and cohabitation. Even the divorce ceremony might be governed by tribal custom.

Contact an attorney who is knowledgeable about the law in your tribal court for legal advice on pursuing a divorce in tribal court or on the requirements for recording a divorce obtained in state court with the clerk of the tribal court.

1.13 Is there a waiting period for a divorce in Nevada?

No. Nevada has no mandatory waiting period. Once residency is established, an uncontested (both parties agree to all terms) divorce can be granted as quickly as a court can act on the paperwork. This can be as quick as a few days to a couple of weeks.

1.14 What is a *divorce complaint*?

A *divorce complaint,* also referred to as a *complaint for divorce,* is a document signed by the *plaintiff,* the person filing for divorce, and filed with the clerk of the court to initiate the divorce process. Referred to as a *petition* in some other states, the complaint sets forth in very general terms what the plaintiff is asking the court to order. An example follows.

Sample Divorce Complaint

DISTRICT COURT
FAMILY DIVISION
CLARK COUNTY, NEVADA

JANE DOE,
Plaintiff,

CASE NO:
vs. DEPT. NO:

JOHN DOE,
Defendant,

DATE OF HEARING:
TIME OF HEARING:

COMPLAINT FOR DIVORCE

Plaintiff, Jane Doe, by and through her attorneys, the Willick Law Group, as and for a cause of action, alleges as follows:

1. Jane is now, and for more than six weeks prior to the commencement of this action has been, a *bona fide* resident of Clark County, Nevada, having actually and physically resided and been domiciled herein during all relevant periods of time preceding the commencement of this action, except during personal or business travel to other places.
2. Jane and Defendant John Doe were duly and legally married in Riverside, California, on June 28, 1975, and have since been, and now are, husband and wife.
3. There are no remaining minor children of this marriage, and Jane is not now pregnant.
4. There is community property to be divided by this Court, the full extent of which is to be discovered.
5. There is community debt to be divided by this Court, the full extent of which is to be discovered.
6. There is separate property and there are separate debts which should be confirmed to each party.
7. Jane has been out of the workforce for the entirety of the marriage and should be awarded interim spousal support during the pendency of the litigation and alimony—both rehabilitative and permanent—post-divorce.

8. Jane retained counsel for this matter and if this matter is contested, she should receive compensation for her attorney's fees and costs from John.
9. Jane should retain her name of Jane Doe.
10. The parties are incompatible in their tastes, natures, views, likes, and dislikes, which have become so widely separate and divergent that they are incompatible in marriage with no possibility of reconciliation.

WHEREFORE, Jane prays for Judgment against John as follows:

1. That the bonds of matrimony existing between Jane and John be dissolved, the parties be granted an absolute Decree of Divorce, and each of the parties be restored to the status of single, unmarried persons.
2. That the Court adjudicate the division of the community property between the parties.
3. That the Court adjudicate the division of community debt between the parties.
4. That the Court confirm each party's separate assets and debts.
5. That Jane retain the name of Jane Doe.
6. That John pay spousal support to Jane during the pendency of the litigation and pay alimony post-divorce.
7. That John pay Jane's attorney's fees and costs, if the action is contested.
8. That the Court grant such other relief as requested in this Complaint; and
9. For such other and further relief as the Court deems just and proper in the premises.

DATED this ___ day of _____________, 20__.

Respectfully submitted:

____

MARSHAL S. WILLICK, ESQ.
Nevada Bar No. 002515
3591 E. Bonanza Road, Suite 200
Las Vegas, NV 89110-2101
Phone (702) 438-4100
Attorneys for Plaintiff

VERIFICATION

I Jane Doe, am the Plaintiff in the above-entitled action. I have read the above and foregoing *Complaint for Divorce* and know the contents thereof, and the same is true of my own knowledge, except as to those matters therein contained stated upon information and belief, and as to those matter, I believe them to be true.

I declare under penalty of perjury, under the laws of the State of Nevada (NRS 53.045 and 28 U.S.C. § 1746), that the foregoing is true and correct.

EXECUTED this____day of____________,20___

____
JANE DOE

1.15 My spouse said she filed for divorce last week, but my attorney says there's nothing on file at the courthouse. What does it mean to "file for divorce?"

When lawyers use the term "filing" they are ordinarily referring to actually delivering a legal document (such as a complaint) to the clerk of the court at the courthouse. Sometimes a person who has hired a lawyer to begin a divorce action uses the phrase "I've filed for divorce," although no papers have yet been taken to the courthouse to actually start the legal process.

1.16 If we both want a divorce, does it matter to the judge who files?

Usually not. In the eyes of the court, the *plaintiff* (the party who filed the complaint to start the legal process of the divorce) and the *defendant* (the other spouse) are not seen differently because of which party filed.

Some attorneys prefer to file first, because the plaintiff gets to present its case first at trial—before the other side gets to present their case. In civil litigation (as opposed to criminal cases), the plaintiff gets to go first at trial—usually—because the plaintiff has the "burden of going forward." Some attorneys consider this a small advantage.

Your attorney may advise you to file first or to wait until your spouse files, depending upon the overall strategy for your case and your circumstances. For example, if there is a concern that your spouse will begin transferring assets upon learning about your plans for divorce, your attorney might advise you to seek a temporary restraining order to protect against such an action, without giving prior notice to your spouse. However, if you are separated from your spouse but have a beneficial temporary arrangement, your attorney may advise you to wait for your spouse to file.

Allow your attorney to support you in making the decision about whether and when to start the formal legal process by filing a complaint for divorce.

1.17 Is there a way to avoid embarrassing my spouse and not have the sheriff serve him with the divorce papers at his workplace?

Yes. Talk to your lawyer about the option of having your spouse (or your spouse's lawyer) sign a document known as an *acceptance of service.* Having your spouse sign this document and then filing it with the court eliminates the need to have your spouse served at all, permitting the documents to be accepted through the mail or in person.

1.18 Should I sign an acceptance of service even if I don't agree with what my spouse has written in the complaint for divorce?

Signing the acceptance of service does not mean that you agree with anything your spouse has stated in the divorce complaint or anything that your spouse is asking for in the divorce. Signing the acceptance of service only means that you admit getting the documents, and substitutes for having a process server personally hand you those documents. You do not waive the right to object to anything your spouse has stated in the complaint for dissolution of marriage.

Follow your attorney's advice on whether and when to sign an acceptance of service. There may be consequences to signing an acceptance when one party lives in Nevada and the other party lives in another state.

1.19 Should I contact an attorney right away if I have received divorce papers?

Yes. If your spouse has filed for divorce, it is important that you obtain legal advice as soon as possible. Even if you and your spouse are getting along, having independent legal counsel can help you make decisions now that could affect your divorce, and your future, later.

After your spouse has filed for divorce, you only have twenty days in which to file an *answer* (a response to a complaint) and to make a counterclaim. If you miss this deadline, a "default" could be entered against you and you could lose valuable assets and other important matters requested in your spouse's complaint.

1.20 During my divorce, what am I responsible for doing?

Your attorney will explain what actions you should take to further the divorce process and to help you reach the best possible outcome.

You will be asked to:

- Keep in regular contact with your attorney.
- Update your attorney regarding any changes in your contact information, such as your address, phone number, and e-mail address.
- Provide your attorney with all requested documents.
- Be honest in all information given to your attorney.
- Provide requested information in a timely manner.
- Complete forms and questionnaires.
- Appear in court on time.
- Be direct about asking any questions you might have.
- Tell your attorney your thoughts on settlement or what you would like the judge to order in your case.
- Remain respectful toward your spouse throughout the process.
- Comply with any temporary court orders, such as protection or support orders.
- Advise your attorney of any significant developments in your case.

By doing your part in the divorce process, you enable your attorney to partner with you for a better outcome while also lowering your attorney's fees.

1.21 Some of the legal language is confusing. What do the terms being used mean?

Law has a language all its own, and attorneys sometimes lapse into "legalese," forgetting that nonlawyers may not recognize words used daily in the practice of law. Some words and phrases you might hear, and what they mean, include:

- *Dissolution of Marriage*—The divorce
- *Plaintiff*—Person who files the divorce complaint
- *Defendant*—Person who did not file the divorce complaint
- *Jurisdiction*—Authority of a court to make rulings affecting a party. Also, sometimes, means the place of a court decision
- *Service*—Process of notifying a party about a legal filing
- *Discovery*—Process during which each side provides information to the other
- *Decree*—The final order entered in a divorce
- *Community Property*—Generally, property acquired by a husband or wife, or both, during the marriage
- *Separate Property*—Generally, property acquired by either a husband or wife before marriage, and property acquired during marriage by "gift, bequest, devise, descent," or an award for personal injury damages, with the rents, issues, and profits thereof
- *Exclusive Possession*—An order, usually temporary, granting one party the possession, during the case and until further order, of an asset, such as a home or car
- *Temporary Orders*—Usually, orders entered during a divorce case as to any issue, which remain until changed or until a final decree is issued.
- *Notice of Entry (NOE)*—The formal document sent to the court showing that an order has been sent to the other party. This starts various time deadlines.
- *Uniform Child Custody Jurisdiction and Enforcement Act (UCCJEA)*—The law effective in almost every state that determines which court can make an order regarding child custody

- *Uniform Interstate Family Support Act. (UIFSA)*—The law effective in every state that determines which court can make an order regarding child support
- *Court rules*—the Eighth Judicial District Court Rules (Clark County) (EDCR), Washoe County District Court Rules (WDCR), and Nevada Rules of Civil Procedure (NRCP)
- *Temporary Protective Order (TPO)*—An order issued by a hearing master or a judge that can make short-term orders to stay away from the party obtaining the order. It may also provide for custody, possession of a home, or some other matters, and sometimes is issued without notice to the other party.
- *Case Management Conference (CMC)*—A procedural meeting, with the judge, both attorneys, and both parties, to determine how the case will proceed, how long before a trial can be set, and some other matters
- *16.2 Disclosures*—The materials, information, and documents required by the court rules to be turned over to the other party very early on in the case (and supplemented as the case proceeds), even if the other party does not request them
- *Financial Disclosure Form (FDF)*—(previously known as an *AFC,* or *Affidavit of Financial Condition*). The court-approved form required by both sides reporting their income, assets, and expenses
- *Joint Preliminary Injunction (JPI)*—A form of order, often issued at the beginning of a case, generally forbidding either party from harassing the other, removing the children permanently from Nevada, or disposing of any community property without agreement of the other party or court order
- *Qualified Domestic Relations Order (QDRO)*—Technically, this refers only to orders dividing retirement plans by private employers, like those obtained through the culinary union. Some lawyers use the term to refer to any retirement plan division order, including those through the military, the Civil Service, or Nevada Public Employees' Retirement System (PERS).

- *Hague Convention*—While there are several such "conventions" (international treaties), usually the term is used in family law to refer to the treaty dealing with civil remedies for the international kidnaping of children.

Never hesitate to ask your attorney the meaning of any terms being used. It is essential that you understand exactly what is being asked of you and told to you by your attorney. It is part of your attorney's job to explain the meaning of the language used and the legal ramifications for each decision you and your attorney make.

1.22 I'm worried that I won't remember to ask my lawyer about all of the issues in my case. How can I be sure I don't miss anything?

Write down all of the topics you want to discuss with your attorney, including what your goals are for the outcome of the divorce. The sooner you clarify objectives for your divorce, the easier it will be for your attorney to support you to get what you want. Your attorney is likely to think of some issues that you may have forgotten.

Divorce Issues Checklist

- ☐ Dissolution of marriage
- ☐ Custody of minor children
- ☐ Removal of children from jurisdiction
- ☐ Parenting plan (time, schedule, and transportation)
- ☐ Child support
- ☐ Extraordinary expenses
- ☐ Life insurance to secure unpaid child support
- ☐ Automatic withholding for support
- ☐ Child-care expenses
- ☐ Health insurance on minor children
- ☐ Uninsured medical expenses for minor children
- ☐ Private school tuition for children
- ☐ College expenses for children
- ☐ Health insurance on the parties
- ☐ Real property: marital residence
- ☐ Real property: rentals, cabins, commercial property (deed, refinancing, sale)
- ☐ Marital expenses associated with real estate

Divorce Issues Checklist (Continued)

- ☐ Time-shares
- ☐ Retirement plans (401k, simple IRA), possible QDROs
- ☐ Federal, state, or military pensions (FERS, CSRS, TSP), possible COAPs
- ☐ Businesses
- ☐ Bank accounts
- ☐ Investments
- ☐ Stock options
- ☐ *Intangible* property such as patents, copyrights, and trademarks
- ☐ Premarital or nonmarital assets
- ☐ Alimony
- ☐ Pets
- ☐ Personal property division (including motor vehicles, recreational vehicles, campers, airplanes, collections, furniture, electronics, tools, household goods)
- ☐ Exchange date for personal property
- ☐ Division of martial debt
- ☐ Property settlement
- ☐ Life insurance to secure unpaid alimony
- ☐ Sums owed under temporary orders
- ☐ Tax exemptions for minor children
- ☐ IRS Form 8332 for claiming children as dependents
- ☐ Filing status for tax returns for the last/current year
- ☐ Claims for injuries to you or your property (*tort claims*) by your spouse
- ☐ Are there any potentially hidden assets to uncover?
- ☐ Deposits, reimbursements, or receivables
- ☐ Restoration of former name
- ☐ Attorney fees

1.23 My spouse has all of our financial information. How will I be able to prepare for negotiations and trial if I don't know the facts or have the documents?

Once your divorce has been filed with the court and temporary matters have been addressed, your attorney will proceed with a process known as *discovery*.

Through discovery, your attorney can ask your spouse to provide documents and information needed to prepare your case.

1.24 My spouse and I both want our divorce to be amicable. How can we keep it that way?

It is in the best interest of both you and your spouse to remain willing to cooperate while moving through the divorce process. Doing so will make your lives easier and less stressful, and save you money on attorney's fees. It is also more likely to result in an outcome you are both satisfied with.

Find a lawyer who understands your goal to reach settlement and encourage your spouse to do the same. Cooperate with the prompt exchange of necessary information. Ask your attorney about the options of mediation and negotiation for reaching agreement. Even if you are not able to settle all of the issues in your divorce, these actions can increase the likelihood of agreement on many terms, and narrow the scope of what remains contested. This should lower the cost.

1.25 Can I get a different judge?

Talk to your attorney about the reasons you want a different judge as early as possible in the process. Each side of a case is given the opportunity, at the very beginning of a case, to make a "peremptory challenge" of the judicial assignment and a new judge will be assigned. No reason for doing so need be given. There is a cost for doing this, so talk to your lawyer to determine if it is in your best interest.

There may be times your lawyer will use other methods to change judges, but once any ruling has been made, or the time for a peremptory challenge has passed, this can only be done in certain instances and will cost a significant amount of money. If you—or your attorney—have a valid reason for seeking a different judge, it may still be in your best interest to do so.

1.26 How long will it take to get my divorce?

The more you and your spouse are in agreement, the faster your divorce will conclude.

Assuming all issues, such as custody, support, property, and debts, are completely settled between you and your spouse, a final hearing or a summary disposition (submitting divorce papers without going to court at all) can be held fairly quickly.

Of course, if a case is contested it will take much longer. It is not unusual for contested cases to take months or even years to be concluded.

1.27 What is the significance of my divorce being final?

The finality of your divorce decree, sometimes referred to as the *decree of divorce,* is important for many reasons. Among other things, it can affect your right to remarry, your eligibility for health insurance from your former spouse, and your filing status for income taxes.

1.28 When does my divorce become final?

Your divorce becomes final upon filing the *notice of entry of the decree of divorce.* Though temporary orders might be terminated when the decree is filed, other new orders, such as for post-divorce support, or property transfers, or post-divorce custody of children, might go into effect on the date of trial, upon filing the decree, or at other times specified in the decree.

1.29 Can I start using my former name right away and how do I get my name legally restored?

You may begin using your former name as soon as you have a file stamped copy of the *decree of divorce* that states that the name has been changed. Many agencies and institutions will not alter their records without a court order changing your name.

If you want your former name restored, let your attorney know this early in the process so that this provision can be included in your complaint and in your divorce decree. If you want to change your legal name after the divorce and have not provided for it in your decree, it might be necessary for you to file a separate legal action for a name change.

2

Temporary and Final Court Orders

Although an entirely uncontested divorce can be quite fast, any contested case is more of a marathon than a sprint and can last months or even years. Cases in litigation have a beginning, a middle, and an end, as outlined in chapter 1.

Unlike cases on television, in the real world it is not typical for things to be decided in a single, decisive, and dramatic hearing. Rather, there are several phases in a case, and a number of decisions can be made during the case that affect how people live while the divorce is ongoing. In the preliminary phase, positions are taken by the parties and either agreements are reached for how matters of property, debt, income, and custody will be attended to, or the parties are unable to reach such agreements and the court is required to enter orders that are effective during the time the case is ongoing. Such orders can be as major as who lives in the house and cares for the children or as minor as who pays the water bill.

Sometimes those orders are changed, for one reason or another, between the beginning of a case and its conclusion. In the meantime, both sides gather the information they need to resolve the case, by agreement or at trial through discovery, as described in chapter 6. In family law, even after the "final" order is entered, some things can be changed. This chapter explains some of the orders that can be made by a court during and after a divorce case.

2.1 What is an *ex parte* court order?

An *ex parte* court order is obtained by one party going to the judge to ask for something without giving prior notice to, or an opportunity to be heard by, the other side. *Ex parte* orders are generally limited to a few simple procedural matters and emergency situations, such as requests for temporary protection orders.

With the exception of temporary protection orders, a few simple procedural matters, or orders to keep a person from leaving the jurisdiction with children, judges are usually reluctant to sign *ex parte* orders. Ordinarily, the court will require the other side to have notice of any requests for court orders and an opportunity to oppose the requests made, and a hearing will be held.

An *affidavit,* which is a written statement of the facts supporting a request to the court, sworn under oath, is usually required before a judge will sign an *ex parte* order. When an *ex parte* order is granted, the party who did not request the order will usually have an opportunity to have a subsequent hearing before the judge to determine whether the order should remain in effect.

2.2 What do I do if my spouse obtained an *ex parte* order against me?

Usually, if an *ex parte* order has been granted, a hearing will be set at the same time to hear whether it is proper for that order to remain in effect. If not, you can request a hearing to determine whether that order is one that should remain in place, or should be set aside, or otherwise altered.

2.3 What is a *motion*?

A *motion* is a request that the judge enter a court order of some type. If there is a request for some kind of court order before the divorce is finished, it is called a *pretrial motion.* Those after a divorce decree has been entered are *posttrial motions.*

A pretrial motion is the means to obtain temporary orders that remain in effect during the pendency of the divorce case. For example, your attorney may file a written motion with the court right at the beginning of the case asking for temporary custody and child support, temporary exclusive possession of the house, etc. For a great deal of detail on such pretrial motions, see the information posted at http://willicklawgroup.com/preliminary-matters-and-motions/.

Some motions are made to handle certain procedural aspects of your case, such as a motion for a continuance asking that a court date be changed or a motion for extension of time asking that the court extend a deadline. In some cases a motion may be made orally rather than in writing, for example when an issue arises during the course of a court hearing or trial. Usually, a posttrial motion seeks to change something that was set out in the divorce decree.

2.4 Once my complaint for divorce is filed, how soon can a temporary hearing be held to decide what happens with our child and our finances while the divorce is pending?

In most cases a temporary hearing can be held within thirty days of filing a motion asking for temporary orders. A motion can be filed at the same time that a complaint for divorce is filed. In emergencies, attorneys can request an *order shortening time* for an earlier date.

2.5 How much notice will I get if my spouse seeks a temporary order?

It depends. Nevada law requires that you receive "reasonable notice" of any court hearing. The court rules provide that you have ten days from the date you are served in which to oppose the motion. Your spouse will then have an opportunity to reply to your opposition, which is supposed to be filed at least five days before the hearing.

If an order shortening time is requested and granted, however, a hearing could be held as soon as one day after a request for a hearing is filed.

2.6 What is a financial disclosure form and why do I have to fill one out?

If the court hears a motion that concerns money in any way—child support, spousal support, attorney's fees, payment of the mortgage, etc.—*both* parties are required to file financial disclosures on the court-approved forms. This allows the judge to have an idea what the monthly bills are, who has possession of what income and property, and who is paying for what. That information is used by the judge to determine whether the requested orders should be granted and, if so, how much to order a party to pay.

This information is critical to both the court and to your lawyer, so you should start working on your financial disclosure as soon as you can, and make it as complete and accurate as possible. Failure to hand in a complete and accurate financial disclosure—within the time the rules specify to file and serve it on the other side—can cause the court to rule against you, prevent your motion from being heard at all, or even cause the court to award the entirety of omitted property to your spouse.

The financial disclosure forms are changed from time to time, but the current versions should be posted at various places, including http://willicklawgroup.com/preliminary-matters-and-motions/.

2.7 If either my spouse or I file for divorce, will I be ordered out of my home? Who decides who gets to live in the house while we go through the divorce?

Some couples remain living in the same house throughout the divorce process. Others find this too uncomfortable and awkward, and separate during the divorce. If you and your spouse cannot reach an agreement regarding which of you will leave the residence during the divorce, the judge will decide whether one of you should be granted "exclusive possession" of the home until the case is concluded. In some cases judges have been known to refuse to order either party out of the house until the divorce is concluded.

If there are minor children, the custodial parent will ordinarily be awarded temporary possession of the residence, so that the children do not have to relocate. Other factors the judge may consider include:

- Whether one of you owned the home prior to the marriage
- After provisions are made for payment of temporary support, who can afford to remain in the home or obtain other housing

- Who is most likely to be awarded the home in the divorce
- Options available to each of you for other temporary housing, including other homes, friends, or family members who live in the area
- Special needs that would make a move unduly burdensome, such as a health condition or special accommodations in the home
- Self-employment operating out of the home, which could not be readily moved, such as a child-care business

If staying in the home is important to you, talk to your attorney about your reasons so that a strong case can be made for you at the temporary hearing.

2.8 How quickly can I get a divorce in Nevada?

Either you or your spouse must have been a resident of Nevada for at least six weeks (forty-two days) immediately prior to the filing of the complaint for the divorce with the court. Usually, those days must be consecutive—in other words—not a day or week here and there.

A lot more information about the necessary grounds for filing for divorce, and whether the court has jurisdiction to enter a divorce or decide other questions, is discussed in chapter 1 of this book and in the explanation and articles posted on our website at http://willicklawgroup.com/grounds-and-jurisdiction/.

After you file, your divorce, your spouse must be given notice of the divorce. Normally, once the complaint for divorce is filed, your spouse will have twenty days after being served with the paperwork in which to answer the complaint.

If both parties are interested in complete cooperation in the divorce process, the process can be very fast. If everyone is willing to sign off on a proposed decree, the divorce could take just a few days to complete.

However, if your spouse does not cooperate, default would have to be filed, after the time for your spouse to answer expired; that would take, realistically, at least a month from first filing to completion. If your spouse is going to actively oppose you on any issues, including property, child custody, child support, or alimony, the length of time for the divorce could increase dramatically, and the process could take many months, or longer than a year.

Consult an attorney to get possible time estimates based upon your particular set of facts.

2.9 I really need a divorce quickly. Will the divorce I get in another country be valid in Nevada?

That depends. If both you and your spouse cooperate in the divorce action and meet the criteria for a divorce in that country, it is likely it will be recognized in Nevada. Normally, "mail order," "quickie," or "one-party" divorces obtained in foreign countries without participation of one of the spouses (and sometimes without anyone ever being present there at all) are not recognized in the United States, including Nevada.

A good suggestion is to "domesticate" the divorce judgment in Nevada. You will need a certified copy of the judgment and it must be translated into English if necessary. You may also need an *apostille,* a formal international certification from the country where the divorce was obtained.

Contact a qualified lawyer prior to going through the expense of a foreign divorce to ensure it will be acceptable in Nevada. The lawyer will be able to tell you if the orders from that foreign court (such as child-support and child-custody orders) will all be acceptable in Nevada.

3

Coping with Stress during the Divorce Process

It may have been a few years ago. Or, it may have been many years ago. Perhaps it was only months. But, when you said, "I do," you meant it. Like most people getting married, you planned to be a happily married couple for the rest of your life.

But things happen. Life brings change. People change. Whatever the circumstance, you now find yourself considering divorce. The emotions of divorce run from one extreme to another as you journey through the process. You may feel relief and be ready to move on with your life. On the other hand, you may feel emotions that are quite painful. Anger. Fear. Sorrow. Guilt. A deep sense of loss or failure. It is important to find support for coping with all these strong emotions.

Because going through a divorce can be an emotional time, having a clear understanding of the divorce process and what to expect will help you make better decisions. And, when it comes to decision making, search inside yourself to clarify your intentions and goals for the future. Let those intentions be your guide.

3.1 My spouse left home weeks ago. I don't want a divorce because I feel our marriage can be saved. Should I still see an attorney?

It's a good idea to see an attorney. Whether you want a divorce or not, there may be important actions for you to take now to protect your assets, credit, home, children, and future right to support.

Additionally, in the world of no-fault divorce, it might happen whether you want it to or not. Your spouse may already have filed for divorce and be posturing to take advantage of you not being prepared. Or he or she might be about to do so. It is best to be prepared with the support of an attorney, even if you decide not to file for a divorce at this time.

3.2 The thought of going to a lawyer's office to talk about divorce is more than I can bear. I canceled the first appointment I made because I just couldn't do it. What should I do?

Many people going through a divorce are dealing with lawyers for the first time and feel anxious about the experience. Ask a trusted friend or family member to help you prepare. He or she can support you by writing down your questions in advance and making sure you are comfortable before going in to the consultation.

Though many people want to have friends with them in a consultation, this is discouraged as the communications between you and your attorney are protected by the "attorney-client privilege"—which assures what you say in confidence generally cannot be revealed to anyone else. By allowing a third party to hear all the details that you are discussing with your attorney, you are essentially waiving this privilege and this may hurt you in the litigation.

Realize that nothing bad can happen to you at a consultation—the lawyer is there to hear your story and provide you with information about the legal realities facing you. This cannot hurt you, and might very well help you. It is very likely that you will feel greatly relieved just to be better informed.

3.3 There is some information about my marriage that I think my attorney needs, but I'm too embarrassed to discuss it. Must I tell the attorney?

What your lawyer does *not* know may be used to hurt you. If this information is going to come out in the litigation anyway, it is much better that your lawyer know about it in advance. While you may feel uncomfortable for a short moment when you disclose it, it is important that your attorney have complete information so that your interests can be fully protected. If speaking directly about certain facts still seems too hard, consider putting them in a letter to your lawyer.

Attorneys who practice divorce law are accustomed to hearing a lot of intimate information about families. While it is deeply personal to you, it is unlikely that anything you tell your lawyer will be a shock, and it may not even be relevant to the case.

Your attorney has an ethical duty to maintain confidentiality. If this information is not a topic being litigated, past events in your marriage are matters that your lawyer is obligated to keep private.

3.4 I'm unsure about how to tell our children about the divorce, and I'm worried I'll say the wrong thing. What's the best way?

How you talk to your children about the divorce will depend upon their ages and emotion development. Changes in your children's everyday lives, such as a change of residence or one parent leaving the home, are far more important to them.

Simpler answers are best for young children. Avoid giving them more information than they need, or looking to them for emotional support; use the adults in your life as a source of support to meet your own emotional needs.

After the initial discussion, keep the door open to further talks by creating opportunities for them to ask questions or talk about the divorce. Use these times to acknowledge their feelings and offer support. Always assure them that the divorce is not their fault and that they are still loved by both you and your spouse, regardless of the divorce.

Information about legal proceedings and meetings with lawyers are *NOT* to be discussed with the children. Nevada court rules require that you not speak to the children about the divorce proceedings or allow them to see any of the documents that are being filed in court or used in the process. Never leave court papers where a child can find them.

3.5 My youngest child seems very depressed about the divorce, the middle one is angry, and my teenager is skipping school. How can I cope?

A child's reaction to divorce can vary depending upon his or her age, personality, and other factors. Some may cry and beg for a reconciliation, and others may act out. Reducing conflict with your spouse, being a consistent and nurturing parent, and making sure both of you remain involved with your children are all actions that can support them regardless of how they are reacting to the divorce.

There are a number of books intended to assist parents with problems children face during divorce. Support groups for children whose parents are divorcing are also available at many schools and religious communities. A school counselor can also provide support. If more help is needed, confer with a therapist experienced in working with children.

3.6 I am so frustrated by my spouse's "Disneyland parent" behavior. Is there anything I can do to stop this?

Feelings of guilt, competition, or remorse sometimes lead a parent to be tempted to spend parenting time in trips to the toy store and special activities. Other times they can result in an absence of discipline in an effort to become the favored parent or to make the time "special."

Shift your focus from the other parent's behavior to your own, and do your best to be an outstanding parent during this time. This includes keeping a routine for your child for family meals, bedtimes, chores, and homework. Encourage family activities, as well as individual time with each child, when it's possible.

During this time when a child's life is changing, providing a consistent and stable routine in your home can ease his or her anxiety and provide comfort.

3.7 Between requests for information from my spouse's lawyer and my own lawyer, I am totally overwhelmed. How do I manage gathering all of this detailed information by the deadlines imposed?

First, simply get started. Often thinking about a task is worse than doing the job itself.

Second, break it down into smaller tasks. Perhaps one evening you gather your tax returns and on the weekend you work on your monthly living expenses.

Third, let in support. Ask that friend of yours who just loves numbers to come over for an evening with her calculator to help you get organized.

Finally, communicate with your lawyer. Your attorney or the lawyer's paralegal staff may be able to make your job easier by giving you suggestions or help. It may be that essential information can be provided now and the details submitted later.

3.8 I am so depressed about my divorce that I'm having difficulty getting out of bed in the morning to care for my children. What should I do?

See your health care provider. Although feelings of sadness are common during a divorce, more serious depression means it's time to seek some professional support.

Some feelings of depression—and lots of other emotions—are common during a divorce. You should expect to have "highs and lows" throughout the divorce process, and just expecting that might make it easier to cope with such feelings. You also want to make sure that you identify any physical health concerns.

Your health and your ability to care for your children are both essential. Follow through on recommendations by your health care professionals for therapy, medication, or other measures to improve your wellness.

3.9 I know I need help to cope with the stress of the divorce, but I can't afford counseling. What can I do?

You are wise to recognize that divorce is a time for letting in support. You can explore a number of options, including:

- Meeting with a member of the clergy or lay chaplain
- Joining a divorce support group
- Turning to friends and family members
- Going to a therapist or divorce coach. If budget is a concern, contact a social agency that offers counseling services on a sliding fee scale

If none of these options are available, look again at your budget. You may see that counseling is important enough that you decide to find a way to increase your income or lower your expenses to support this investment in your well-being.

3.10 I'm the one who filed for divorce, but I still have loving feelings toward my spouse and feel sad about divorcing. Does this mean I should dismiss my divorce?

Whether or not to proceed with a divorce is a deeply personal decision. Strong feelings of caring about your spouse often persist after a divorce is filed. While feelings can inform us of our thoughts, sometimes they can also cause us to not look clearly at everything there is to see in our situation.

Have you and your spouse participated in marriage counseling? Has your spouse refused to seek treatment for an addiction? Are you worried about the safety of you or your children if you remain in the marriage? Can you envision yourself as financially secure if you remain in this marriage? Is your spouse involved in another relationship?

The answers to these questions can help you get clear about whether to consider reconciliation. Talk to your therapist, coach, or spiritual advisor to help determine the right path for you. But, in any event, do not vacillate and give contradictory signals as your moods change. Where necessary, professional help in these matters is key.

You may have an emotional connection with an ex-spouse for the rest of your life. An old saying is that "the opposite of love is not hate; it is indifference." You may never hate your ex-spouse, even if that is what you should be feeling, and it is perfectly natural for your feelings about your ex-spouse to change over time—hopefully, for the better as time and distance lessen intensity.

3.11 Will my lawyer charge me for the time I spend talking about my feelings about my spouse and my divorce?

The quick answer is yes. When you are paying your attorney by the hour, expect to be charged for the time your attorney spends talking with you no matter the subject. Generally, lawyers are not therapists, and you should use other resources for emotional support.

3.12 My lawyer doesn't seem to realize how difficult my divorce is for me. How can I get him to understand?

Everyone wants compassion and validation from the professionals who help during a divorce. Speak frankly with your attorney about your concerns. It may be that your lawyer does not see your concerns as being relevant to the job of getting your desired outcome in the divorce. Your willingness to improve the communication will help your lawyer understand how best to support you in the process and will help you understand which matters are best left for discussion with your therapist or a supportive friend.

Remember, you have an attorney for representation, not commiseration, and you have hired the lawyer to take the emotion out of the process because acting on emotion usually results in bad decisions. Having an empathetic attorney is good, but an attorney can only function properly when maintaining a degree of professional objectivity. An attorney who takes on a client's problems as his or her own is dangerous to you both.

3.13 I've been told not to speak ill of my spouse in front of my child, but I know my spouse is doing this all the time. Why can't I just speak the truth?

It can be devastating for your child to hear you badmouthing his or her other parent. What your child needs is permission to love both of you, regardless of any bad parental behavior. The best way to support your child during this time is to encourage a positive relationship with the other parent.

3.14 Nobody in our family has ever been divorced and I feel really ashamed. Will my children feel the same way?

Your family is not ending, it is changing. Making a change in how you see your family identity is huge for you. The best way to help your children is to establish a sense of pride in their new family configuration and to look forward to the future with a real sense of possibility.

Your children will have an opportunity to witness you overcoming obstacles, demonstrating independence, and moving forward in your life notwithstanding challenges. You can be a great teacher to them during this time by demonstrating pride in your family and in yourself.

3.15 I am terrified of having my deposition taken. My spouse's lawyer is very aggressive, and I'm afraid I'm going to say something that will hurt my case.

A deposition is an opportunity for your spouse's attorney to gather information and to assess the type of witness you will be if the case proceeds to trial. Feeling anxious about your deposition is normal. However, regardless of the personality of the lawyers, most depositions in divorces are quite uneventful.

A deposition is not a place to try to convince the other side of the correctness of your positions, or to argue. Generally, you should simply answer the questions asked, without volunteering any further information. "I don't know" and "I don't remember" are acceptable answers—if true.

Remember that your attorney will be seated by your side at all times to support you, and to object to questions, or behavior, by the other side that violate court rules or ethical guidelines. Ask to meet with your lawyer in advance to prepare for the deposition. If you are worried about certain questions that might be asked, talk to your attorney about them. Think of a deposition as an opportunity, and enlist your lawyer's support in being well prepared.

3.16 I am still so angry at my spouse; how can I be expected to sit in the same room during a settlement conference?

If you are still really angry at your spouse, it may be beneficial to postpone the conference for a time. You might also consider seeking some counseling to support you with coping with your feelings of anger.

Another option might be "shuttle" negotiations. With this method, you and your attorney remain in one room while your spouse and his or her attorney are in another. Settlement offers are then relayed between the attorneys throughout the negotiation process. By shifting your focus from your angry feelings to your goal of a settlement, it may be easier to proceed through the process.

3.17 I'm afraid I can't make it through court without having an emotional breakdown. How do I prepare?

A divorce trial can be a highly emotional time, calling for lots of support. Some of these ideas may help you through the process:

- Meet with your lawyer or the firm's support staff in advance of your court date to prepare you for court.
- Ask your lawyer whether there are any documents you should review in preparation for court, such as your deposition.
- Visit the courtroom in advance to get comfortable with the surroundings.
- Ask your lawyer about having a support person with you on your court date.
- Ask yourself what is the worst thing that could happen and consider what options you would have if it did.
- Avoid alcohol, eat healthfully, exercise, and have plenty of rest during the period of time leading up to the court date. Each of these will help you to prepare for the emotions of the day.
- Plan what you intend to wear in advance. Small preparations will lower your stress.

- Visualize the experience going well. Picture yourself sitting in the witness chair, giving clear, confident, and truthful answers to easy questions.
- Arrive early in the courthouse and make sure you have a plan for parking your car if you are not familiar with the area.
- Take slow, deep breaths. Breathing deeply will steady your voice, calm your nerves, and improve your focus.

Your attorney will be prepared to support you throughout the proceedings. By taking the above steps, you can increase the ease of your experience.

3.18 I am really confused. One day I think I've made a mistake, the next day I know I can't go back, and a few minutes later I can hardly wait to be single again. Some days I just don't believe I'm getting divorced. What's happening?

Shock, denial, anger, bargaining, depression and acceptance are common passages for a person going through a divorce. One moment you might feel excited about your future and a few hours later you think your life is ruined. This is all perfectly normal, and natural.

What can be helpful to remember is that you may not pass from one stage to the next in a direct line. Feelings of anger or sadness may well up in you long after you thought you had moved on. Similarly, your mood might feel bright one day as you think about your future plans, even though you still miss your spouse.

Taking good care of yourself is essential; what you are going through requires a tremendous amount of energy. Allow yourself to experience your emotions, but also continue moving forward. These steps will help your life get easier day by day.

Winston Churchill once said: "When you are going through hell, keep going." The important thing to realize is that divorce is a process that at some point will end. The emotional stress will lessen with time. Be as patient as you can, and remember that there is life after divorce.

4

Working with an Attorney

If there is one thing you can be sure of in your divorce, it's that you will be given plenty of advice. Well-intentioned neighbors, cousins, and complete strangers will be happy to tell you war stories about their ex or about their sister who got divorced in Canada fifteen years ago. Many will insist they know what you should do, even though they know nothing about the facts of your case or the law in Nevada or how it will apply to your case.

But there is one person whose advice will—and should—matter to you: your attorney. Your lawyer should be your trusted and supportive advocate at all times throughout your divorce. The counsel of your attorney can affect your life for years to come. You will never regret taking the time and energy to choose the right lawyer for you. Generally, making that choice entails conversations with multiple prospective attorneys. It is essential that you select an attorney with whom you feel comfortable.

You should see your relationship with your attorney as a partnership for pursuing what is most important to you. To arrive at this result, you cannot be afraid to ask questions. Asking questions is the means to clear and open attorney-client communication, which, in turn, leads to understandable, if not always agreeable, results.

4.1 Where do I begin looking for an attorney for my divorce?

There are many ways to find a divorce lawyer. To start, ask people you trust—friends and family members who have gone through a divorce—if they thought they had a great lawyer (or if their former spouse did!). If you know professionals who work with attorneys (such as CPAs, psychologists, or appraisers), ask for a referral to an attorney who is experienced in family law.

In Nevada, the state bar provides two useful services. First, the bar posts a list of certified family law specialists. See www.nvbar.org/content/certified-specialists. To be qualified as a family law specialist, an attorney must have practiced in the field of family law for at least five years, obtained a significant amount of specialized education (called *Continuing Legal Education,* or *CLE*), and passed the required family law certification exam.

Second, the bar lists useful biographical information on each attorney, including year of admission of practice and whether the lawyer maintains professional liability (i.e., malpractice) insurance, and provides a contact to the state bar's disciplinary office so you can check to see if a lawyer you are considering has a history of professional discipline actions being taken by the bar.

Consult your local bar association to find out whether it has a referral service. Some counties do, but some counties don't have such a service. Be sure to specify that you are looking for an attorney who handles divorces.

Check with the William S. Boyd School of Law at the University of Nevada, Las Vegas. A faculty member may be able to recommend a qualified lawyer in your area.

Go online. Many attorneys have websites that provide information on their practice areas, professional associations, experience, and philosophy. Our website, www.willicklawgroup.com, provides a substantial amount of information on nearly every aspect of family law, as well as extensive information about this firm and its lawyers.

There are certain specialty organizations for family law attorneys with strict admission standards as to experience and ability. Probably the most well known and reputable of these is the American Academy of Matrimonial Lawyers, at AAML.org (search for lawyers who are members of the organization at http://aaml.org/find-a-lawyer).

There are also third-party "rating" sites available. Currently, the most often referenced sites are those run by the Martindale-Hubbell service, and the AVVO Internet service.

Martindale-Hubbell mainly relies on "peer reviews"—the service sends out surveys to other lawyers and judges to get ratings for lawyers. If possible, you will want to find a family law attorney who is "A/V" rated—meaning that other lawyers and judges have rated that attorney as being very high to pre-eminent in skill, with very high ethics. The service has two main sites: Martindale.com (search for lawyers at www.martindale.com/Find-Lawyers-and-Law-Firms.aspx) and Lawyers.com (search for lawyers at www.lawyers.com/).

AVVO mainly relies on a proprietary computer algorithm to rank lawyers on the basis of public information. Its website and information can be found at avvo.com (search for lawyers at www.avvo.com/find-a-lawyer).

As with most things on the Internet, you should take whatever you find with a grain of salt—it is possible for anyone with a grudge to post false and even defamatory information about a lawyer. So do not assume that anything you read about a lawyer posted by some other person—good or bad—is necessarily true.

4.2 How do I choose the right attorney?

Choosing the right attorney for your divorce is an important decision. Your attorney should be a trusted professional with whom you feel comfortable sharing information openly. He or she should also zealously advocate on your behalf within the confines of the rules and procedures that govern attorney conduct.

You will rely upon your attorney to help you make many decisions throughout the course of your divorce. You will also entrust your legal counsel to make a range of strategic and procedural decisions on your behalf. Do not be afraid to request an explanation for any of these choices and actions.

Generally, your first meeting with your attorney will be at a formal "consultation." It is important to remember that your attorney is there to not only inform you of the law and what to expect from the legal process, but to answer your questions about all related matters that will support your decisions.

Feel free to seek all information you need to help you make an informed decision, but remember that your lawyer will only be able to provide legal support. If what you need is psychological counseling, you can ask for referrals, but your lawyer is probably not the proper person for that task. You will probably have lower costs, and better results, if you use mental health professionals or friends and family as emotional sounding boards. Your time and money spent with your lawyer should be dedicated to things that your lawyer can actually accomplish.

Find an attorney who practices primarily in the family law area. While many attorneys "do divorces," and any licensed attorney can attempt to do so, you will likely have more effective representation at a lower ultimate cost from an attorney who already knows the substance and procedure of Nevada divorce law.

Determine the level of experience you want in your attorney. For example, if you have a short marriage with no children and few assets, an attorney with less experience might be a good value for your legal needs. However, if you are anticipating a custody dispute, or have complex or substantial assets, a more experienced attorney may better meet your needs.

Consider the qualities in an attorney that are important to you. Even the most experienced and skilled attorney is not right for every client. Ask yourself what you are really looking for in an attorney so you can make your choice with developed standards in mind, and feel free to ask questions.

As with most things, it is generally easier and far less expensive to get all aspects of your divorce proceeding right the first time than to try to fix errors and omissions after the fact. Finding a competent and knowledgeable lawyer at the outset is your best bet to eliminate, to the extent possible, having to face future proceedings after the divorce on the basis of procedural or legal errors.

It is important that you are confident in the attorney you hire. If you're unsure about whether the lawyer is really listening to you or understanding your concerns, keep looking until you find one who does. Your divorce is an important matter. It's critical that you have a professional you can trust.

4.3 Should I interview more than one attorney?

Be willing to interview more than one attorney. Every lawyer has different strengths, and a different personality, and it is important that you find the one that is right for you. Sometimes it is only by meeting with more than one attorney that you see clearly who will best be able to help you reach your goals in the way you want.

Because most lawyers charge for consultations, there can be a significant cost to multiple consultations. But, if possible, you should do whatever is necessary to be comfortable that you are making the right choice. Changing lawyers in the middle of litigation can be stressful and costly, as a new attorney will need to get caught up on the history of your case. It is wise to invest your energy and time at the outset to find a lawyer who is right for you.

4.4 My spouse says since we're still friends we should use the same attorney for the divorce. Is this a good idea?

No. Even the most amicable of divorcing couples usually have differing interests. In most cases, an attorney is ethically prohibited from representing two people with conflicting interests who are in dispute. For this reason, it is never recommended that an attorney represent both parties to a divorce.

Sometimes couples reach agreements without understanding all of their rights under the law, or even knowing what issues are actually at stake. A person facing divorce often will benefit from receiving independent legal advice on matters such as tax considerations, retirement, and health insurance issues. If at all possible, you want to be able to ask questions of an attorney whose only duty is to your interests in the case.

It is not uncommon for one party to retain an attorney and for the other party not to do so. In such cases, the party with the attorney files the complaint, and any agreements reached between the parties are typically written up and sent to the unrepresented spouse for approval prior to any court hearing.

If your spouse has filed for divorce and said that you do not need an attorney, you should nevertheless meet with a lawyer for advice on how proceeding without a lawyer could affect your legal rights and to review any paperwork that has been sent to you. Sometimes, the important thing is not what a document says, but what it does not say. While lawyers are trained to look for such issues, most people without legal training are not usually equipped to do so.

4.5 What information should I take with me to the first meeting with my attorney?

Attorneys differ on the amount of information they like to see at an initial consultation. Most attorneys ask you to complete a detailed questionnaire at the time of your first meeting. Ask whether it is possible to do this in advance of your meeting. This can allow you to provide more complete information and to make the most of your appointment time with the lawyer. To make this easier, some firms post their initial questionnaire on their websites; ours is posted at http://willicklawgroup.com/consultation-policies/.

If you or your spouse have already filed any papers with the court for divorce, a protection order, or otherwise, it is important to bring copies of any such court documents with you. If you ever signed a premarital or postnuptial agreement, that is another important document for you to bring for review.

It is often very useful to have a "chronology," or "time line" of events leading up to the current dispute; sometimes we ask for an outline of the entire relationship. Sometimes it is just as important to know what led to a problem as it is to know the details of the problem itself. Events from months or years earlier can determine the outcome of many different kinds of issues, from jurisdiction to child custody to alimony.

A time line is just a tool to gain an understanding of your case as efficiently and quickly as possible. Usually, they are not very detailed. For a posted explanation of what a time line is and some pointers on how to organize and draft one, see "What to Provide in a 'Chronology' or 'Time Line' of Events," posted at http://willicklawgroup.com/consultation-policies/.

If you intend to ask for support, either for yourself or for your children, documents evidencing income of both you and your spouse may be useful. These might include:

- Recent pay stubs
- Individual and business tax returns, W-2s, and 1099s
- Bank statements showing deposits
- A statement of your monthly budget
- The court's financial disclosure form, filled out by one or both parties

At an initial consultation there is usually not enough time for a detailed review of such documents, but if an economic question comes up during the consultation, having such documents at hand may make it possible to give a much better answer to the question.

If your situation is urgent or you do not have access to any of the documents mentioned above, don't let it stop you from scheduling your appointment with an attorney. Prompt legal advice about your rights is often more important than having detailed financial information in the beginning. Your attorney can explain to you the options for obtaining records if they are not readily available to you.

4.6 What unfamiliar words might an attorney use at the first meeting, and what do they mean?

Law has a language all its own. Some of the terms, abbreviations, and references a lawyer might make during a consultation, or in later discussions, are explained in chapter 1 of this book. Sometimes, lawyers use the rule numbers, or the names of published cases, as shorthand references for procedures or requirements. Never hesitate to ask your attorney the meaning of any terms used by him, the opposing attorney, or the judge. In order for you to make decisions and give directions to your attorney, it is necessary that you understand the terms being used and what they mean to you.

4.7 What can I expect at an initial consultation with an attorney?

The nature of the advice you get from an attorney in an initial consultation will depend upon what stage you are in when you meet—whether you are still deciding whether you want a divorce, are planning for a possible divorce in the future, are ready to file for divorce right away, or are already involved in divorce litigation.

During the meeting, you should be prepared to provide the following information to the attorney:

- A brief history of the marriage
- Background information regarding yourself, your spouse, and your children
- Your immediate situation
- Your intentions and goals regarding your relationship with your spouse
- What information you are seeking from the attorney during the consultation

You can expect the attorney to provide the following information to you:

- The procedure for divorce in Nevada
- A preliminary list of the issues important in your case
- A preliminary assessment of your rights and responsibilities under the law
- Background information regarding the firm
- Information about the attorney's fees and office procedures
- Information concerning filing fees and court costs

The initial consultation is an opportunity for you to ask all of the questions you have at the time of the meeting. Some questions may be impossible for the attorney to answer at that time because additional information or research is needed. The intent is for you to leave that first meeting knowing the answer to questions that are knowable, knowing the range of possible outcomes for those things that can be estimated, and knowing what information or developments are necessary to answer your remaining questions.

It is important to remember that no attorney can—or ever should—guarantee you a result. There is almost always some doubt as to outcomes. The legal process involves people, and people, including judges, are fallible. Anyone involved can see things differently, or make mistakes, even when it seems to you that the evidence mandates a different result.

4.8 Is what I say at a consultation kept confidential?

With few exceptions, attorneys are required to keep confidential all information you provide. The privilege applies to any information you give to your attorney or a member of the attorney's staff, such as secretaries and paralegals.

There are certain rare exceptions. For example, an attorney might be required to reveal information necessary to prevent death or substantial bodily harm. Also, information provided by someone pretending to seek legal advice, for the purpose of disqualifying the lawyer, is generally considered nonconfidential.

If you have any questions about the scope of the attorney-client privilege, they should be discussed at the beginning of the consultation and before revealing whatever information you have questions about.

4.9 Can I bring a friend or family member to my initial consultation?

Yes, but it does raise a possible complication.

Having someone present during your initial consultation can be a source of great support and comfort. You might ask the person accompanying you to take notes on your behalf so that you can focus on listening and asking questions. Sometimes, the person you wish to bring has valuable information, or specific questions, that would be helpful to you in deciding what to do.

However, the "attorney-client privilege"—which recognizes the confidentiality of nearly all communications between you and an attorney—does not extend to a third party present during your consultation. This means that your friend or family member could potentially be called to testify as to what was disclosed during your initial consultation, or otherwise be asked to testify whether you have ever said or admitted something.

Generally, if you are going to disclose information not already known by whoever you wish to bring to a consultation, and you have any concern about that information, you should ask the attorney privately whether it should be discussed with your friend or family member present, before doing so.

4.10 What exactly will my attorney do to help me get a divorce?

Your attorney will play a critical role in helping you get your divorce. You will be actively involved in some of the work; although other actions, such as legal research at the law office or court house, will not require your presence.

Your attorney may perform any of the following tasks on your behalf:

- Determine which court has jurisdiction to hear your divorce, or any of the issues relating to your divorce.
- Develop a strategy for advising you about all aspects of your divorce, including the treatment of assets and matters concerning children.
- Prepare legal documents for filing with the court.
- Conduct discovery to obtain information from the other party, which could include depositions, requests for production of documents, requests for admissions, and written interrogatories.
- Appear with you at court appearances, depositions, and conferences.
- Schedule all deadlines and court appearances.
- Support you in responding to information requests from your spouse.
- Inform you of actions you are required to take.
- Perform financial analyses of your case.
- Determine and discuss with you the possibility of utilizing the services of an expert to help deal with certain aspects of your case.
- Conduct legal research.

- Prepare you for court appearances and depositions.
- Prepare your case for hearings and trial, including preparing exhibits, creating outlines, and interviewing witnesses.
- Advise you regarding your rights under the law, and your options as the case progresses.
- Counsel you regarding the risks and benefits of negotiated settlement or other "alternate dispute resolution" processes, as compared to proceeding to trial.

As your advocate, your attorney is entrusted to take all of the steps necessary to represent you and protect your interests in the divorce.

4.11 What professionals might the court appoint to work with my attorney?

It depends on what sorts of issues are present in your case. In some cases where custody or parenting time issues are seriously disputed, the court may appoint a *guardian ad litem (GAL)*; that is, a representative (who may or may not be a lawyer) whose duty it is to represent the best interest of the child. The guidelines for such GALs are in flux, but such a person may have the responsibility to investigate you and your spouse as well as the needs of your child. Sometimes, the GAL may submit reports to the court, or be called as a witness at trial to testify regarding any relevant observations.

In some child-custody cases, the court appoints a psychologist for one of several possible roles. For example, the psychologist may be appointed to perform a child-custody evaluation, which involves assessing both parents and the child, or may be ordered to evaluate one parent to assess the child's safety while spending time with that parent.

In cases that involve complex or unclear financial issues, the court may appoint a forensic expert to determine the value of a business, the extent of a community estate, and/or research an allegation of marital waste. Such an expert is typically a CPA or professional business appraiser.

There are times where the court will appoint a *special master* to perform an investigation or draft a report on some issue important to the case, such as the value of retirement benefits, or to determine how much of an asset is actually community property.

4.12 I've been divorced before and I don't think I need an attorney this time; however, my spouse is hiring one. Is it wise to act as my own lawyer?

Having gone through a prior divorce, it's likely that you have learned a great deal about the divorce process as well as your legal rights. However, there are many reasons why you should be extremely cautious about proceeding without legal representation.

It is important to remember that every divorce is different. The length of the marriage, whether there are children, the relative financial situation for you and your spouse, the specific assets (and debts) involved, as well as your age and health can all affect the outcome in your divorce.

You may not even know of all the issues actually presented by your current circumstances. For example, few people not trained in the subject know how the availability of making changes to survivorship benefits in some retirement plans changes upon actual retirement. There could be issues that were mostly irrelevant at age forty that are far more critical at sixty-five.

The law may have changed since your last divorce. New laws get passed by the Nevada legislature and new decisions get handed down by the Nevada Supreme Court that affect the rights and responsibilities of people who divorce.

In some cases the involvement of a lawyer can be minimal—perhaps only to draft the relevant paperwork— but you owe it to yourself to at least discuss your impending case with an attorney to determine the extent of your rights and potential obligations, and to be sure you know of all issues actually present. At a minimum, have an initial consultation with him or her to discuss your rights and have an attorney review any final agreement.

Making informed decisions is critical to obtaining, at the very least, a tolerable outcome in your divorce proceeding, regardless of what is at stake. Having competent professional advice is often critical to minimizing the chance of an unpleasant surprise during or after divorce as to an issue or choice that was overlooked or mistaken during the divorce process. Some things, once they go wrong, cannot be fixed.

4.13 Can I bring my children to meetings with my attorney?

It's best to make other arrangements for your children when you meet with your attorney. Your attorney will be giving you a great deal of important information during your conferences, and it will benefit you to give your full attention.

It's also recommended that you take every measure to keep information about the legal aspects of your divorce away from your children—for example, don't leave court documents laying around your house, and don't speak to your attorney within listening distance of your children. Court rules require keeping this information away from the children, and violations of those rules can lead to sanctions.

Besides, it is just good parenting to follow those guidelines. Not only can knowledge that you are seeing an attorney regarding a divorce add to your child's anxiety about the process, it can also make your child a target for questioning by the other parent about your contacts with your attorney and can lead to issues with the court. Additionally, having children present could breach the attorney-client privilege. Your policy should be to leave the children out of the divorce process as much as possible.

In any event, most law offices are not designed to accommodate young children and are ordinarily not "child-proof." For both your child's well-being and your own peace of mind, explore options for having someone care for your children when you have meetings with your attorney.

Note that most courts do not allow minor children to be present at the courthouse for any court hearing or trial.

4.14 What is the role of the *paralegal* or *legal assistant* in my attorney's office?

A *paralegal,* or *legal assistant,* is a nonlawyer but is a trained legal professional whose duties include providing support for you and your lawyer. The exact roles paralegals serve vary from office to office, but typically they help with information gathering, reviewing documents with you, providing you with updates on your case, and preparing documents for attorney review and filing.

Paralegals also often answer your questions about the divorce process and developments in your case that do not call for legal advice; these are essentially the "who, what, where, and when" questions that come up in nearly every case. The "why" questions are generally left to your attorney. This is because a paralegal is prohibited by the ethical codes and court rules from giving legal advice.

It is important that you respect the limits of the role of the paralegal. Do not get frustrated or angry if a paralegal is unable to answer your question because it calls for a legal opinion; if you get such a response, it means that the paralegal is doing the job correctly. However, a paralegal can answer many questions and provide a great deal of information to you throughout your divorce.

Working with a paralegal can make your divorce easier because he or she is likely to be more easily available to help you. Communicating with paralegal staff can also lower your legal costs, as the hourly rate for paralegal services is almost always less than the rate for attorneys.

4.15 My attorney is not returning my phone calls. What can I do?

You have a right to expect your phone calls and written messages to be returned by your lawyer; indeed, "communication" is one of the first rules of professional conduct governing attorney behavior. However, it is important to remember that you are probably not the only client your attorney has, and sometimes lawyers are required by other cases—or perhaps your case—to be in court for days at a time, or otherwise temporarily unavailable.

At your initial consultation, it is a good idea to discuss your lawyer's protocol for returning calls and messages. Many offices have a policy of returning all calls or messages within one or two business days—others have different policies. Some offices send regular status reports whether or not anything notable is happening in a case. Others do not. Knowing the rules that apply in your lawyer's office can reduce frustration on both sides.

It is also good to remember that "life happens." Lawyers and their staff members, like other people, have illnesses, injuries, family emergencies, vacations, and holidays, all of which can slow response times upon occasion. The key is to be reasonable and temper expectations as to responses to your inquiries within the rules you and your lawyer agree to follow.

If you are having problems in getting responses to requests for information, however, consider some of these options:

- First make sure your messages have been received, rather than being lost, misdirected, or going to spam.
- Ask to speak to the paralegal or another attorney in the office.
- Send an e-mail or fax telling your lawyer that you have been trying to reach him or her by phone and explaining the reason it is important that you receive a call.
- Ask the receptionist to schedule a phone conference for you to speak with your attorney at a specific date and time, and keep the appointment.
- Schedule a meeting with your attorney to discuss both the issue needing attention as well as your concerns about the communication.

Your attorney wants to provide good service to you. If your calls and messages are not being returned, take action to get communications with your lawyer back on track.

4.16 How do I know when it's time to change lawyers?

Changing lawyers is costly, and sometimes can injure your case; it is not a step to take lightly. You will incur legal fees for your new attorney to review information that is already familiar to your current attorney. You will spend time giving much of the same information to your new lawyer that you gave to the one you have discharged. A change in lawyers often results in delays in the divorce process to allow your new attorney to catch up on all that has occurred in your case.

The following are questions you should ask yourself when you're deciding whether to stay with your current attorney or seek new counsel:

- Have I spoken directly to my attorney about my concerns?
- When I expressed concerns, did my lawyer take action accordingly?
- Is my lawyer open and receptive to what I have to say?
- Am I blaming my lawyer for bad behavior of my spouse or opposing counsel?
- Do I believe my attorney is competent to handle my case?
- Have I provided my lawyer the information needed for taking the next action?
- Does my lawyer really have control over my grievances, or are they simply the result of the law on a given subject, outcomes that would have been the same no matter who my lawyer was, or a judge's unpredictable action?
- Is my lawyer keeping promises for completing actions on my case?
- Do I trust my lawyer?
- Is my lawyer actually advocating on my behalf?
- Do I believe my lawyer will support me to achieve the outcome I'm seeking in my divorce?
- What would be the advantages of changing lawyers compared to the cost; is there something that a new lawyer could do that my current lawyer cannot do?

As these questions illustrate, you should make every effort to resolve concerns with your current attorney prior to changing counsel.

However, if you are considering changing counsel, these are probably good steps to follow:

- Make an appointment with your lawyer, and have a list with you of specific concerns and problems to address, to see if you can resolve them, or perhaps discover that they can't be resolved.
- Make a "second-opinion consultation" appointment with another lawyer. It may be that the second law-

yer's analysis will give you food for thought or a perspective you had not thought of. On the other hand, the lawyer may confirm your concerns that something is in fact wrong with your current attorney-client relationship.

- Write out the "pros" and "cons" of changing lawyers, including matters of cost, time lost, and where you are in the progress of your case.

In the event your current attorney does not or cannot resolve your concerns for one reason or another, and you think your case may be better handled by another office, it may be time to switch attorneys.

5

Attorney's Fees and Costs

Any time you make a major investment, you want to know what the cost is going to be and what you are getting for your money. Investing in quality legal representation for your divorce is no different.

The cost of your divorce might be one of your greatest concerns. Because of this, you will want to be an intelligent consumer of legal services. You want quality, but you also want to get the best value for the fees you are paying.

Legal fees for a divorce can be costly and the total expense is not always predictable. But there are many actions you can take to estimate the cost in advance, and to control the cost as the case goes on.

Develop a plan early on for how you will finance your divorce. Speak openly with your lawyer about fees from the outset. Learn as much as you can about how and how much you will be charged. Find out if your case will be done on a flat fee (this is uncommon) or on an hourly basis and whether you will have an *initial retainer* or a *renewable retainer* (commonly called an *evergreen retainer*). Insist on a *written fee agreement,* and on understanding every aspect of what you will be charged.

Being informed, aware, and wise is the best way of doing what you can to make your financial investment in your divorce money well spent to protect your future.

5.1 Can I get free legal advice from a lawyer over the phone?

Every law firm has its own policy regarding lawyers talking to people who are not yet clients of the firm. Most questions about your divorce are too complex for a lawyer to give a meaningful answer during a brief phone call, beyond the most basic matters applicable to every case.

Getting reliable and specific answers to your questions about your divorce requires a complete look at the facts, circumstances, and background of your marriage. To obtain good legal advice, it's best to schedule an initial consultation with a lawyer who handles divorces.

5.2 Will I be charged for an initial consultation with a lawyer?

It depends. Some lawyers give free consultations as a "loss leader" to their practices, while others charge a fee. When scheduling your appointment, you should be told the amount of the fee in advance. Payment is ordinarily due at the time of the consultation.

5.3 Will I be expected to give money to the attorney after our first meeting? If so, how much?

If your attorney charges for an initial consultation, be prepared to make payment at the time of your meeting. At the close of your consultation, the attorney may tell you the amount of the retainer needed by the law firm to handle your divorce. The retainer is paid after you have decided to hire the lawyer, the lawyer has accepted your case, and you are ready to proceed.

5.4 What exactly is a *retainer* and how much will mine be?

The word has had different meanings over the years. In Nevada today, a *retainer* is usually a deposit paid to your lawyer in advance for services to be performed and costs to be incurred in your divorce. This will be either an amount paid toward a "flat fee" for your divorce, or (much more commonly) an advance deposit of money to pay for services that will be charged by the hour.

If your case is accepted by the law firm, expect the attorney to request a retainer before work begins on your case. The amount of the retainer may vary from hundreds of dollars to several thousand dollars, depending upon the nature of your case, and the policies of the law office. Divorces involving contested custody, businesses, or interstate disputes, for example, are all likely to require higher retainers.

Probably the most important question in terms of how much a case will cost is just how much the parties to the case are determined to fight about whatever issues exist in the case, rather than working together to solve them. The more contested a case appears to be, the higher the retainer will usually be. Other factors that can affect the amount of the retainer include the nature and number of the disputed issues.

5.5 I don't have any money and I need a divorce. What are my options?

Two factors to consider in your situation are time and money.

If your income is very low and your assets are few, you may be eligible to obtain a divorce lawyer to assist you at no cost or minimal cost through the Legal Aid Center of Southern Nevada (if you live in Clark County), Washoe Legal Services (if you live in Northern Nevada), or Volunteer Attorneys for Rural Nevadans (if you live in rural Northern or Central Nevada). You may also qualify for a free or reduced-retainer lawyer through the Nevada State Bar Association Lawyer Referral Service. Such lawyer services are called *pro bono.*

These organizations have a screening process for potential clients, as well as limits on the nature of the cases they take. The demand for their services is also usually greater than the number of attorneys available to handle cases. If you are eligible for legal services from one of these programs, you should anticipate being on a waiting list.

For the truly indigent, most courts have fee waivers available for even the filing fee. You have to ask for such a waiver. A *pro bono* lawyer should know how to make an application for a fee waiver.

In short, if you have very little income and few assets, you are likely to experience some delay in obtaining a lawyer.

If you believe you might be eligible for participation in one of these programs, inquire as early as possible to increase your opportunity to get the legal help you are seeking.

5.6 I don't have much money, but I need to get a divorce as quickly as possible. What should I do?

If you have *some* money and want to divorce as soon as possible, consider some of these options:

- Borrow the legal fees.
- Charge the legal fees on a low-interest credit card.
- Talk to your attorney about using money held in a joint account with your spouse.
- Find an attorney who will work with you on a monthly payment basis.
- Ask your attorney about your spouse paying for your legal fees.

Contact the Legal Aid Center of Southern Nevada, Washoe Legal Services, or Volunteer Attorneys for Rural Nevada and let them know you have some ability to pay and ask for help finding a lawyer who will take your case for a reduced fee.

Even if you do not have the financial resources to proceed with your divorce at this time, you should consult with an attorney to learn your rights and to develop an action plan for steps you can take between now and the time you are able to proceed. Planning ahead can sometimes save you massive headaches and heartaches in the future, not to mention a lot of money in the long run.

Often, there are measures you can take right away to protect yourself until you have the money to proceed with your divorce.

5.7 Can I hire a lawyer on *contingency* to represent me in my divorce?

The short answer is "no." A *contingency fee* is one in which the lawyer agrees to do the work in exchange for a portion of the recovery obtained. This is most frequently seen in personal injury actions (for example, in auto accident cases). A simple example of a contingency fee is that the lawyer would receive, for example, one-third of any recovery obtained. If such a case resulted in a $10,000 settlement, the lawyer would receive $3,333, and the rest would go to the client.

Under the current ethical rules governing all lawyers, however, contingency fee agreements are prohibited in "a domestic relations matter, the payment or amount of which is contingent upon the securing of the divorce or upon alimony, child support, or property settlement in lieu thereof." In other words, no one is allowed to hire a lawyer on a contingency fee basis to prosecute or defend a divorce case involving any of those issues.

It is sometimes possible to hire a lawyer on contingency in some cases that come out of divorce cases, though. For example, if there had already been a divorce, and one party owed the other party money for a property settlement, or even child support, but did not pay it, the party who is owed the money could hire a lawyer on a contingency basis to collect the *arrearages* (past-due payments).

In other words, contingency fees are permissible in domestic relations actions to collect past-due payments (so long as the fee is reasonable, any fees awarded are credited against the contingency fee, and the client was advised of the options of hiring counsel hourly or seeking services from the district attorney's office). Also, contingency fees are acceptable in actions to modify property settlements "independent of support issues."

It is possible that this rule will change in the future, because the Nevada Supreme Court has stated that the rule "does raise some concerns with respect to certain individuals' ability to retain an attorney in domestic relations cases." But until the rule is changed (if it ever is), no lawyer in Nevada can take a divorce case on a contingency fee basis.

5.8 Is there anything I can do on my own to get support for my children if I don't have money for a lawyer for a divorce?

Yes. If you need support for your children, contact the Child Support Division of the Clark County District Attorney's Office for help in obtaining a child-support order. If you live in Northern Nevada, contact the Washoe County District Attorney for assistance. Although they cannot help you with matters such as custody or property division, they can pursue support from your spouse for your children.

Don't be surprised if you are asked lots of questions about where the children are currently residing and for how long. Jurisdiction for ordering or modifying a child-support order must be determined before a court can act.

5.9 How much does it cost to get a divorce?

The cost of your divorce will depend upon many factors. Some attorneys complete divorces for a "flat fee," but most charge by the hour. A *flat fee* is a fixed amount for the legal services being provided. It is more likely to be used when there are no children of the marriage and the parties have agreed upon the division of their property and debts. Most Nevada attorneys charge by the hour for divorces because it is usually difficult to tell how much time and effort will be required to complete the case.

It is important that your discussion of the cost of your divorce begin at your first meeting with your attorney. It is customary for family law attorneys to request a retainer, also known as a fee advance, prior to beginning work on your case. Planning for paying an attorney must take into consideration replenishment of the retainer as funds are used in your case.

Be sure to ask your attorney what portion, if any, of the retainer is refundable if the case is finished quickly, if you do not continue with the case, or if you terminate your relationship with the attorney. You should note that a "non-refundable retainer" is not authorized in Nevada, so make sure you understand if any of the retainer is considered a flat fee for some of the work to be performed.

5.10 What are typical hourly rates for a divorce lawyer?

In Nevada in recent years, attorneys who practice in the divorce area often charge from $125 per hour to well over $500 per hour. The rate your attorney charges may depend upon factors such as the skills, reputation, and experience of that lawyer, and what other attorneys in the area are charging.

It is common for more-experienced attorneys in a firm to have a higher hourly rate than more-junior attorneys in the firm, who are usually called *associates*. If you have a concern about an attorney's hourly rate, but you would like to hire that attorney's firm, consider asking to work with an associate attorney in the firm who is likely to charge a lower rate. Associates are often supervised and trained by the senior partners, and many are fully capable of handling your case.

5.11 Can I make payments to my attorney?

Every law firm has its own policies regarding payment arrangements for divorce clients. Sometimes these arrangements can be tailored to the specific client, but most law firms have policies of some sort as to how they handle such requests.

Most attorneys will require a substantial retainer to be paid at the outset of your case. Some attorneys may accept monthly payments instead, or take a very small retainer followed by monthly payments. Others may require additional retainers as your case progresses. Ask frank questions of your attorney until you clearly understand your responsibility for payment of legal fees.

5.12 I agreed to pay my attorney a substantial retainer to begin my case. Will I still have to make monthly payments?

Ask your attorney what will be expected of you regarding payments on your account while the divorce is in progress. Get clear on whether monthly payments on your account will be expected, whether it is likely that you will be asked to pay additional retainers, and whether the firm charges interest on past-due accounts. Regular payments to your attorney can help you avoid having a tremendously burdensome legal bill at the end of your case. Your written retainer agreement should clearly detail all of these provisions.

5.13 I've been turned down by programs providing free legal services. How can I get the money to pay for a lawyer?

There are a number of options to consider when it seems as though you are without funds to pay an attorney.

First, ask yourself whether you have closely examined all sources of funds readily available to you. Sometimes, people simply overlook money that they might be able to access with ease. Consider taking out a loan or charging your retainer on a credit card.

Next, talk to your family members and friends. Often, those close to you are concerned about your future and would be willing to support you in your goal of having your rights protected. While it may be uncomfortable to ask for a loan, remember that most family and friends will appreciate that you trusted them enough to ask for their help. If the retainer is too much money to request from a single individual, consider whether several persons might each be able to contribute a lesser amount to help you hire a lawyer.

If your case is not urgent, consider developing a plan for saving the money you need to proceed with a divorce. Your attorney may be willing to receive and hold monthly payments until you have paid an amount sufficient to pay the initial retainer.

Under certain circumstances, an attorney might be willing to be paid from the proceeds of a property settlement. If you and your spouse have acquired substantial assets during the marriage, you may be able to find an attorney who will wait to be paid until the assets are divided at the conclusion of the divorce. But don't count on this possibility; lawyers, like most people, do not want to have payment for their work depend on uncertain outcomes.

5.14 My lawyer gave me an estimate of the cost of my divorce and it sounds reasonable. Do I still need a written fee agreement?

Absolutely. Insist upon a written agreement with your attorney. This is essential not only to define the scope of the services for which you have hired your lawyer, but also to ensure that you have clarity about matters such as your attorney's hourly rate, whether you will be billed for certain costs such as copying, and when you can expect to receive statements on your account.

A clear fee agreement reduces the risk of misunderstandings between you and your lawyer. It supports you both in being clear about your promises to one another so that your focus can be on the legal services being provided rather than on disputes about fees or costs. Our retainer agreement, which has been used as a model by various firms, is posted on our website at various places, including at http://willicklawgroup.com/fees-costs/.

5.15 How will I know how the fees and charges are accumulating?

Be sure your written fee agreement with your attorney is completely clear about how you will be informed regarding the status of your account.

If your attorney agrees to handle your divorce for a flat fee, your fee agreement should clearly set forth what is included in the fee.

Most attorneys charge by the hour for handling divorces. At the outset of your case, be sure your written fee agreement includes a provision for the attorney to provide you with regular statements of your account. It is reasonable to ask that these be provided at least monthly. It is usually best to receive these statements via e-mail. You should establish a secure e-mail address to which no other person has access. This will ensure a quick way for you and your attorney or his staff to communicate with you.

Review the statement of your account promptly after you receive it. Check to make sure there are no errors, such as duplicate billing entries. If your statement reflects work that you did not know was being done, call for clarification. Your attorney's office should welcome any questions you have about what services it is providing, and why.

Your statement might also include filing fees, court reporter fees for transcripts of court testimony or depositions, copy expenses, or interest charged on your account.

If several weeks have passed and you have not received a statement on your account, call your attorney's office to request one. Legal fees can mount quickly, and it is important that you stay aware of the status of your legal expenses.

5.16 What other expenses are related to the divorce litigation besides lawyer fees?

Talk to your attorney about costs other than the attorney's fees. There can be a lot of possible expenses in a divorce case, depending on the issues involved. Ask whether it is likely there will be filing fees, court reporter expenses, subpoenas, depositions, appraisal, examination, testing, or expert witness fees. Expert-witness fees can be a substantial expense, usually in the thousands of dollars, depending upon the type of expert and the extent to which the expert is involved in your case.

Speak frankly with your attorney about these costs so that together you can make the best decisions about how to use your budget for the litigation.

5.17 Who pays for the experts such as appraisers, accountants, and psychologists?

Costs for the services of experts, whether appointed by the court or hired by the parties, are ordinarily paid for by the parties.

The judge can order these fees to be shared equally by the parties. However, depending upon the circumstances, one party can be ordered to pay the entire fee or cost, or the cost can be divided in a different proportion than equally.

Psychologists either charge by the hour or set a flat fee for certain types of evaluations. Again, the court can order one party to pay this fee or both parties to share the expense. It is not uncommon for a psychologist to request payment in advance and hold the release of an expert report until fees are paid.

The fees for many experts, including appraisers and accountants, will vary depending upon whether the individuals are called upon to provide only a specific service such as an appraisal, or whether they will need to prepare for giving testimony and appear as a witness at trial.

A property appraiser's fees can vary significantly depending on what is being appraised. Residential property is usually the cheapest kind of property on which to get an appraisal; raw land and commercial property are usually much more expensive to appraise.

Talk to your attorney about these costs so you are aware of what to expect.

5.18 What factors will impact how much my divorce will cost?

While it is difficult to predict how much your legal fees will be, the following are some of the factors that affect the cost:

- Whether there are children
- Whether child custody is agreed upon
- Whether there are novel legal questions
- Whether a pension plan will be divided between the parties
- The nature of the issues being contested, and the evidence required
- The number of issues agreed to by the parties
- The cooperation of the opposing party and opposing counsel
- Whether there are litigation costs, such as fees for expert witnesses or court reporters
- The hourly rate of the attorney
- Who the assigned judge is on your case
- Your (and the other party's) willingness to negotiate settlement

Communicating with your lawyer regularly about your legal fees will help you to have a better understanding of the overall cost as your case proceeds, and may help you have a hand in determining and controlling those costs.

5.19 Will my attorney charge for phone calls and e-mails?

Unless your case is being handled on a flat-fee basis, you should expect to be billed for phone calls and e-mails to and from your attorney. Many of the professional services provided by lawyers are done by phone and by e-mail. This time can be spent giving legal advice, in negotiation, or gathering information to protect your interests. These calls and e-mails are all legal services for which you should anticipate being charged by your attorney.

To make the most of your time during attorney phone calls, plan your call in advance. Organize the information you want to relay, your questions, and any concerns to be addressed. Write a checklist if that is helpful to you in staying organized. Being clear and focused during each phone call will help ensure that your fees are well spent.

The same goes for any e-mails that you intend to send to your lawyer. Don't send a string of one-question e-mails when you can include all of your questions in one e-mail, and try to be as organized, and to the point, as possible in all such e-mails. This will save you considerable money in the long run.

5.20 Will I be charged for talking to the staff at my lawyer's office?

It depends. Check the terms of your fee agreement with your lawyer. Whether you are charged for talking to non-lawyer members of the law office may depend upon their role in the office. For example, many law firms charge by the hour for the services of paralegals and law clerks, but not for receptionists or some administrative staff.

Remember that nonlawyers cannot give legal advice, and respect their roles. Don't expect the receptionist or a paralegal to give you an opinion regarding whether you will win custody or receive alimony.

Your lawyer's support staff will be able to relay your messages and receive information from you. They may also be able to answer many of your questions, especially those questions that are "operational" rather than substantive. For example, a paralegal assigned to a case should know when hearings are calendared, or whether filings have been made in a case. Allowing support from non-attorneys in the firm is one of the ways to control your legal fees.

5.21 What is a *litigation budget,* and how do I know if I need one?

If your case is complex and you are anticipating substantial legal fees, ask your attorney to prepare a *litigation budget* for your review. Such a budget projects what costs are expected in a case, and for what future tasks.

This can help you to understand the nature of the services anticipated, the time that may be spent, and the overall cost. It can also be helpful for budgeting and planning for additional retainers. Knowing the anticipated costs of litigation can help you to make meaningful decisions about which issues to litigate and which to consider resolving through settlement negotiations.

Different cases or hearings have very different costs, because what needs to be done varies per case. The example below is intended to show the various kinds of tasks that can be budgeted. The numbers given are for demonstration only.

Sample Attorney Litigation Budget

The following example is an approximation of fees and cost, based on assumptions and information given during the consultation process, and is our best guess as to our potential cost in handling this case.

MILITARY RETIREMENT (MRB) AND RELATED ISSUES, FEES, AND COSTS ESTIMATIONS

CASE NAME: SMITH	adv.	JONES
DESCRIPTION	**HOURS**	**EXPENSES**
Legal Services Averaged @ $350.00 per hour; Based on: Partner @ $500.00 per hour Associates @ $350.00 per hour Paralegals @ $125.00 per hour	4	$1,400.00
Pleadings, preparation of stipulations and proposed orders	6	$2,100.00
Preparation for Hearings (Assume 2 hours preparation time for each hour of court/deposition time.)	6	$2,100.00
Attendance at Hearings (Assuming at least one hour of court time for each issue, custody/visitation, asset/debts, alimony, temporary support, preliminary fees, temporary possession, etc.) (Each hearing lasts between 2 and 4 hours)	3	$1,050.00
Discovery Compliance	0	$0.00
Request for Production	0	$0.00
Expert Interrogatories (Business Valuator)	0	$0.00
Request for Admissions	0	$0.00
Telephone Conferences/Correspondence	2	$700.00
Witness Conferences	0	$0.00
Expert Conferences (Business Valuator)	0	$0.00

Sample Attorney Litigation Budget (Continued)

DESCRIPTION	HOURS	EXPENSES
Depositions Preparation, Attendance/taking)	4	$1,400.00
Wife	2	$1,100.00
Husband	2	$1,100.00
Experts (Business Valuator)	0	$0.00
Witnesses	0	$0.00
Friends	0	$0.00
Other family members	0	$0.00
Police/Social workers	0	$0.00
Legal research/memorandum of facts of law	1	$350.00
Trial Preparation	4	$1,400.00
Witness preparation/direct	2	$700.00
Cross-examination	2	$700.00
Summaries, Exhibits	2	$700.00
Trial notebooks	2	$700.00
Trial Brief	4	$1,400.00
7.27 Brief	4	$1,400.00
Trial (one days/10 hours per day)	4	$1,400.00
Preparation of proposed final judgment	2	$700.00
TOTAL	**61**	**$19,000.00**

5.22 What is a *trial retainer* and will I have to pay one?

A *trial retainer* is a sum of money paid on your account with your lawyer when it appears as though your case may not settle and may be proceeding to trial. The purpose of the trial retainer is to fund the work needed to prepare for trial and for services the day or days of trial.

Confirm with your attorney that any unearned portion of your trial retainer will be refunded if your case settles, or if the trial costs proves to be less expensive than anticipated. Ask your lawyer in advance whether and when a trial retainer might be required in your case so that you can avoid surprises and plan your budget accordingly.

5.23 How do I know whether I should spend the attorney's fees my lawyer says it will require to take my case to trial?

Deciding whether to take a case to trial or to settle is often the most challenging task in the divorce process. This decision should be made with the support of your attorney.

When the issues in dispute are mostly financial, often the decision about settlement is related to the costs of going to trial. Your attorney might call this a "cost/benefit analysis." Get clear about just how far apart you and your spouse are on the financial matters and compare this to the estimated costs of going to trial. You also need to gain some sense of the likelihood of winning on each issue in contest. By comparing these amounts, you can decide whether a compromise on some or all financial issues and having certainty about the outcome would be better than paying legal fees to go to trial and not knowing until the trial is over how your case will resolve.

5.24 If my mother pays my legal fees, will my lawyer give her private information about my divorce?

If someone other than you is paying your legal bills, it is important that you are clear with your lawyer and with the person paying that you expect your lawyer to honor the ethical duty to maintain confidentiality. Without your permission, your attorney should not disclose information to others about your case.

If you do want your lawyer to be able to communicate with your family members, advise your lawyer. Expect to be charged by your lawyer for the time spent on these calls or meetings. Regardless of the opinions of the person who pays your attorney fees, your lawyer's duty is to remain *your* advocate.

5.25 Can I ask the court to order my spouse to pay my attorney's fees?

Yes. If you want to ask the court to order your spouse to pay any portion of your legal fees, be sure to discuss this with your attorney at the first opportunity. Most lawyers will treat the obligation for your legal fees as yours until the other party has made payment.

If your case is likely to require costly experts and your spouse has a much greater ability to pay these expenses than you do, talk to your lawyer about the possibility of filing a motion with the court asking your spouse to pay toward these costs while the case is pending.

A lot more information about fees, costs, and when one party might be made to pay the fees of the other side is discussed in the explanation and articles posted on our website at http://willicklawgroup.com/fees-costs/.

5.26 What happens if I don't pay my attorney the fees I promised to pay?

The ethical rules for lawyers allow your attorney to withdraw from your case if you do not comply with your fee agreement. Consequently, it is important that you keep the promises you have made regarding your account.

If you are having difficulty paying your attorney's fees, talk with your attorney about payment options. Consider borrowing the funds, using your credit card, or asking for help from friends and family.

Above all, do not avoid communication with your attorney if you are having challenges making payment. Keeping in touch with your attorney is essential for you to have an advocate at all stages of your divorce.

5.27 Is there any way I can reduce some of the expenses of getting a divorce?

Litigation of any kind can be expensive, and divorces are no exception. The good news is that there are many ways that you can help control the expenses. Here are some of them.

Put it in writing. If you need to relay information that is important but not urgent, consider providing it to your attorney by e-mail. This creates a prompt and accurate record for your file and your lawyer's file in less time than it usually takes to exchange phone messages and talk on the phone.

Keep your attorney informed. Just as your attorney should keep you up to date on the status of your case, you need to do the same. Keep your lawyer advised about any major developments in your life such as plans to move, having someone move into your home, a change in your employment status, or buying or selling property.

During a divorce, your address, phone number, or e-mail address may change. Be sure to let your attorney know immediately. Often, timely advice on the part of your lawyer can avoid the need for more costly fees later.

Obtain copies of documents. An important part of litigation includes reviewing documents such as tax returns, account statements, report cards, or medical records. Your attorney will ordinarily be able to request or subpoena these items, but many may be readily available to you directly upon request.

Consult your attorney's website. If your lawyer has a website, it may be a great source of useful information. The answers to commonly asked questions about the divorce process and procedure can often be found there. The Willick Law Group maintains an extensive website that is used by many litigants and other attorneys as a source of information. You can review this site at www.willicklawgroup.com.

Utilize support professionals. Get to know the support staff at your lawyer's office. The receptionist, paralegal, legal secretary, or law clerk may have the answer to your question. Only the attorneys in the office are able to give you legal advice, but other professionals in the law office can often provide answers to questions regarding the status of your case. These professionals can also relay information from your attorney to you at a much lower cost than you speaking directly to the attorney. Just as with your direct communication with your attorney, all communication with any staff in a law firm is required to be kept strictly confidential.

Consider working with an associate attorney. Although the senior attorneys or partners in a law firm may have more experience, you may find that working with an associate attorney on some or all tasks in a case is a good option. Hourly rates for an associate attorney are typically lower than those charged by a senior partner. Frequently, the associate attorney has trained under a senior partner and developed excellent skills as well as knowledge of the law. Many associate attorneys are also very experienced.

Discuss with the firm the benefits of working with a senior or an associate attorney in light of the nature of your case, the expertise of the respective attorneys, and the potential cost savings to you.

Some firms work as a team and you may find multiple attorneys or staff members are working on your case. This is usually done to maximize the usefulness to you of the expertise of the firm's staff and to keep costs down for you, by having tasks performed as efficiently as possible. If you think this method might work well in your case, talk frankly with your attorney or with that firm's administrator.

Leave a detailed message. If your attorney knows what information you are seeking, the lawyer can often get the answer before returning your call. This not only gets your answer faster, but also reduces costs.

Discuss more than one matter during a call. It is not unusual for clients to have many questions during litigation. If your question is not urgent, consider waiting to call until you have more than one inquiry. However, never hesitate to call to ask any necessary legal questions.

Provide timely responses to information requests. Whenever possible, provide information requested by your lawyer in a timely manner. This avoids the cost of follow-up requests or actions by your lawyer and the additional expense of extending the time in litigation.

Carefully review your statements. Scrutinize your billing statements closely. If you believe an error has been made, contact your lawyer's office right away to discuss your concerns.

Remain open to settlement. Be alert to recognize when your disagreement with your spouse is about smaller sums of money that will cost more in legal fees to take to court than the value of what is disputed.

By doing your part, you can use your legal fees wisely and control the costs of your divorce.

6

The Discovery Process

Interrogatories. Depositions. Subpoena *duces tecum*. Even the words sound foreign.

Discovery is one of the least talked about steps in divorce, but it is often among the most important. The discovery process enables you and your spouse to meet on a more level playing field when it comes to settling your case or taking it to trial.

You and your spouse both need the same information if you hope to reach a fair agreement on the issues in your divorce. Similarly, the judge must know all of the facts to make a fair decision.

The purpose of discovery is to ensure that both you and your spouse have access to the same information. In this way, you can either negotiate a fair agreement or have all of the facts and documents to present to the judge at trial.

The discovery process may seem tedious at times because of the need to obtain and to provide lots of detailed information. Completing it, however, can give tremendous clarity about the issues in your divorce. Trust your lawyer's advice about the importance of having the necessary evidence as you complete the discovery process in order to reach your goals in your divorce.

6.1 What is *discovery*, and is it necessary?

Discovery is that part of your divorce process in which the attorneys attempt to learn as much about the facts of your case as possible. Through a variety of methods, both lawyers will request information from you, your spouse, and potential witnesses in your case.

The court rules have been amended several times in an effort to require as much relevant information as possible to be automatically supplied by both sides at the beginning of the case, and as the case progresses. Unfortunately, not everyone complies with those rules, and sometimes lawyers want or need information beyond that which is provided by the other side under those rules, so traditional discovery is very often still used in divorce cases.

6.2 What types of discovery might be done by my lawyer or my spouse's lawyer?

Types of discovery include:

- *Interrogatories*—written questions that must be answered under oath
- *Requests for production of documents*—asking that certain documents be provided by you or your spouse
- *Requests for admissions*—asking that certain facts be admitted or denied
- *Subpoena of documents*
- *Depositions*—in which questions are asked and answered in the presence of a court reporter, or video-recorded before a notary public or other official authorized to issue oaths, but outside the presence of a judge

Factors that can influence the type of discovery conducted in your divorce can include:

- The types of issues in dispute
- How much access you and your spouse have to needed information
- The level of cooperation in sharing information
- The budget available for performing discovery

Talk to your lawyer about the nature and extent of discovery anticipated in your case.

6.3 How long does the discovery process take?

Discovery can take anywhere from a few weeks to many months, mostly depending on the kind of information needed and how difficult it is to obtain. Also relevant are factors such as the complexity of the case, the cooperation of you and your spouse, and whether expert witnesses are involved.

The Nevada Rules of Discovery provide that interrogatories, requests for production of documents, and requests for admissions be responded to within thirty days of being served. But it is typical for information received to lead to further questions, and for there to be several rounds of discovery.

6.4 My lawyer insists that we conduct discovery, but I don't want to spend the time and money on it. Is it really necessary?

Maybe. The discovery process can be critical to a successful outcome in your case for several reasons:

- It increases the likelihood that any agreements reached are based on accurate information.
- It provides necessary information for deciding whether to settle or proceed to trial.
- It supports the preparation of defenses by providing information regarding your spouse's actual condition, needs, abilities, and care.
- It avoids surprises at trial, such as unexpected witness testimony.

Discuss with your attorney the intention behind the discovery being conducted in your case to ensure it is consistent with your goals and a meaningful investment of your legal fees.

6.5 I just received from my spouse's attorney interrogatories and requests that I produce documents. My lawyer wants me to respond within two weeks. I'll never make the deadline. What can I do?

Answering your discovery promptly will help move your case forward and help control your legal fees. There are steps you can take to make this task easier.

First, look at all of the questions. Many of them will not apply or your answers will be a simple "yes," or "no."

Ask a friend to help you. It is important that you develop the practice of letting responsible people help you while you are going through your divorce. Chances are that you will make great progress in just a couple of hours with a friend helping you.

Break it down into smaller tasks. If you answer just a few questions a day, the job will not be so overwhelming.

Call your lawyer. If you can answer almost everything, but need more time for some particular question or task, tell your lawyer that. Ask whether a paralegal in the office can help you organize the needed information or determine whether some of it can be provided at a later date.

Delay in the discovery process often leads to frustration by clients and lawyers. Do your best to provide the information in a timely manner with the help of others. Doing so will make it a lot easier for your lawyer to request that the other side also responds promptly to your requests.

If you absolutely cannot comply with the deadline provided, advise your lawyer of that fact as far in advance of the deadline as possible, explain why, and ask whether an extension can be obtained.

6.6 My spouse's lawyer intends to subpoena my medical records. Aren't these private?

Maybe. Whether or not your medical records are relevant in your case will depend upon the issues in dispute. If you are requesting alimony or if your health is an issue in a dispute of child custody, these records might be relevant.

Talk with your lawyer about your rights. It may be that a motion to stop the subpoena, known as a *motion to quash,* is needed, or that the records that can be obtained should be limited to those relevant to your divorce.

6.7 It's been two months since my lawyer sent interrogatories to my spouse, and we still don't have his answers. I answered mine on time. Is there anything that can be done to speed up the process?

Probably, if you wish to do so. The failure or refusal of a spouse to follow the rules of discovery can add to both the frustration and expense of the divorce process.

Talk with your attorney about filing a *motion to compel.* This seeks a court order that your spouse must provide the requested information by a certain date. A request that your spouse pay your attorney's fees needed for the filing of the motion may also be appropriate, but you should realize that getting an order for such a payment, or its being made even if ordered, is not a certainty.

Ask your lawyer whether a subpoena of information from an employer or a financial institution would be a more cost-effective way to get needed facts and documents if your spouse remains uncooperative.

6.8 What is a *deposition*?

A *deposition* is the asking and answering of questions under oath, outside of court. The process is in the presence of a court reporter, or video-recorded in front of a notary public or other official authorized to take oaths. A deposition may be taken of you, your spouse, or potential witnesses in your divorce case, including experts. Both attorneys will usually be present. You and your spouse also have the right to be present during the taking of depositions in your case.

Depositions are not performed in every divorce. They are most common in cases involving contested custody, complex financial issues, and expert witnesses.

After your deposition is completed, the questions and answers will sometimes be transcribed, that is, typed by the court reporter exactly as given and bound into one or more volumes.

Depositions can be expensive. In addition to the cost of the court reporter (both for attending and for producing the transcript of the questions and answers), there is the cost of the attorneys to prepare for the deposition and attend a process that can take many hours, or sometimes days.

If the deposition is taken on video, the original is sealed for the court and a copy is used to pick out the relevant testimony that needs to be transcribed. This method is relatively new and is not permitted in all states, but it is available in Nevada and is often a less expensive method than having a court reporter transcribe the entire deposition.

6.9 What is the purpose of a deposition?

A deposition can serve a number of purposes, such as:

- Supporting the settlement process by providing valuable information
- Helping your attorney determine who to use as witnesses at trial
- Aiding in the assessment of the credibility of a witness —that is, whether the witness appears to be telling the truth
- Helping avoid surprises at the trial by learning the testimony of witnesses in advance
- Preserving testimony in the event the witness becomes unavailable for trial

Depositions can be essential tools in a divorce, especially when a case is likely to proceed to trial.

6.10 Will what I say in my deposition be used against me when we go to court?

Perhaps. Usually, a deposition is used to develop trial strategy and obtain information in preparation for trial. In some circumstances, a deposition may be used at trial.

If you are called later to testify as a witness and you give testimony contrary to what you said at your deposition, your deposition can be used to *impeach* you by showing the inconsistency in your statements. This could cause you to lose credibility with the court.

It is important to review your deposition prior to your live testimony to ensure consistency and prepare yourself for the type of questions you may be asked.

6.11 Will the judge read the depositions?

Unless a witness becomes unavailable for trial or gives conflicting testimony at trial, it is unlikely that the judge will ever read the deposition transcripts.

6.12 How should I prepare for my deposition??

To prepare for your deposition, review the important documents in your case, such as the complaint, your answers to interrogatories, and your financial affidavit.

Gather all documents you've been asked to provide at your deposition. Deliver them to your attorney in advance of your deposition for copying and review. Talk to your attorney about the type of questions you can expect to be asked. Discuss with him or her any questions you are concerned about answering.

6.13 What will I be asked? Can I refuse to answer questions?

Questions in a deposition can cover a broad range of topics including your education, work, income, and family. The attorney is allowed to ask anything that is "reasonably calculated to lead to the discovery of admissible evidence." In other words, if the question might lead to relevant information, it can be asked in a deposition, even though that particular question or answer might be inadmissible at trial. If you are unsure whether to answer a question, ask your lawyer and follow his or her advice.

Your attorney also may object to inappropriate questions. If there is an objection, say nothing until the attorneys discuss the objection. You will be directed whether or not to answer.

6.14 What if I give incorrect information in my deposition?

You will be under oath during your deposition, so it is very important that you be truthful. If you give incorrect information by mistake, contact your attorney as soon as you realize the error. Most errors can be easily corrected during the review of the transcript. On the other hand, if you lie during your deposition, you risk being impeached by the other lawyer during your divorce trial. This could cause you to lose credibility with the court, rendering your testimony less valuable.

6.15 What if I don't know or can't remember the answer to a question?

You may be asked questions about which you have no knowledge. It is acceptable to say "I don't know" if the truthful response is that you do not have the knowledge. Similarly, if you cannot remember, simply say so.

6.16 What else do I need to know about having my deposition taken?

The following suggestions will help you to give a successful deposition:

- Prepare for your deposition by reviewing and providing necessary documents and talking with your lawyer.
- Get a good night's sleep the night before. Eat a meal with protein to sustain your energy, as the length of depositions can vary.
- Arrive early for your deposition so that you have time to get comfortable with your surroundings.
- Relax. You are going to be asked questions about matters you're familiar with. Your deposition is likely to begin with routine matters such as your educational and work history.
- Tell the truth, including whether you have met with an attorney or discussed preparation for the deposition. If you are asked whether you talked to your lawyer about the deposition, and you did so, say that if you are asked. There is nothing in the world wrong with talking with your lawyer about the deposition or any other subject matter.
- Stay calm. Your spouse's lawyer will be judging your credibility and demeanor. Do not argue with the attorneys, or attempt to persuade them to change their mind about their view of the case. There may be a time and place to have such a conversation, but a deposition is not such a place.
- Listen carefully to the entire question, and be sure you understand it before answering. Do not try to anticipate questions or start thinking about your answer before the attorney has finished asking the question.
- Answer the question directly. If the question calls only for "yes" or "no," provide such an answer, and then stop talking.

- Do not volunteer information. If the lawyer wants to elicit more information, the he or she will do so in following questions.
- If you are not sure that you understand the question clearly, ask that it be repeated or rephrased. Do not try to answer what you *think* was asked or intended. Focus on what was actually asked. By the same token, don't try to be tricky or creative by interpreting questions otherwise than as asked.
- Take your time and carefully consider the question before answering. There is no need to hurry.
- If you do not know or cannot remember the answer, say so. That is usually an adequate answer.
- Do not guess. If your answer is an estimate or approximation, say so. Do not let an attorney pin you down to anything you are not sure about. For example, if you cannot remember the number of times an event occurred, say that. If the attorney asks you if it was more than ten times, answer only if you can. If you can provide a range (more than ten but less than twenty) with reasonable certainty, you may do so. If you cannot honestly do so, do not do so.
- If an attorney mischaracterizes something you said earlier, say so.
- Speak clearly and loudly enough for everyone to hear you, but resist the urge to yell at anyone, no matter what questions are being asked.
- Answer all questions with words, rather than gestures or sounds. "Uh huh" is difficult for the court reporter to distinguish from "unh unh" and may result in inaccuracies in the transcript.
- If you need a break at any point in the deposition, you have the right to request one. You can talk to your attorney during such a break.
- Discuss with your lawyer in advance of your deposition whether you should review the transcript of your deposition for its accuracy or whether you should waive your right to review and sign the deposition.

Remember that the purpose of your deposition is to support a good outcome in your case. Completing it will help your case to move forward.

6.17 Are depositions always necessary? Does every witness have to be deposed?

Depositions are less likely to be needed if you and your spouse are reaching agreement on most of the facts in your case and you are moving toward a settlement. They are more likely to be needed in cases where child custody is disputed, where there are complex financial issues, or where one party is alleging that things are missing or have been misrepresented.

Although it is very uncommon for depositions of all witnesses to be taken, it is common to take depositions of expert witnesses.

6.18 Will I get a copy of the depositions in my case?

Ask your attorney for copies of the depositions in your case. It will be important for you to carefully review your deposition if your case proceeds to trial.

7

Negotiation, Mediation, and Settlement Conferences

If your marriage was full of conflict, you might be asking how you can make the fighting stop. You picture your divorce looking like a scene from a movie or television drama complete with vicious lawyers and screaming matches. You wonder if there is a way out of this nightmare.

Or, perhaps you and your spouse are parting ways amicably. While you are in disagreement about how your divorce should be settled, you are clear that you want the process to be respectful and without hostility. You'd rather spend your hard-earned money on your children's college education than legal fees.

In either case, going to trial and having a judge make all of the decisions in your divorce is not inevitable. In fact, most Nevada divorce cases can and do settle without a trial.

Direct negotiation, or mediation with a mediator, can help you and your spouse resolve your disputed issues and reach your own agreements without taking your case before a judge who will make your decisions for you.

Resolving your divorce through a negotiated or mediated settlement has many advantages. You can achieve a mutually satisfactory agreement, a known outcome, little risk of appeal, and often enjoy significantly lower legal fees. Despite the circumstances that led to the end of your marriage, it might be possible for your divorce to conclude peacefully with the help of these tools.

7.1 What is the difference between *negotiation* and *mediation*?

Both negotiation and mediation are methods used to help you and your spouse settle your divorce by reaching agreement rather than going to trial and having the judge make decisions for you. These methods (and some others) are sometimes referred to as *alternative dispute resolution,* or *ADR.*

Negotiation is either between the parties to a case directly, or (more often) involves lawyers for both you and your spouse attempting to reach a resolution of the disputes, either in conversations, or in correspondence. Any discussions might, or might not, include the parties personally.

Mediation uses a trained mediator, who is an independent, neutral third party. Usually, a mediator is a skilled professional whose job is to guide the parties through the process of trying to reach agreement on one or more points. Lawyers for the spouses may also be present during mediation, although their involvement is usually less than in negotiation.

Parties can always agree to hire (and pay) a private mediator. As discussed below, some courts have put into place mediation programs as part of the court process.

Different Nevada courts have different rules for what may be mediated in the courts' own mediation programs, and the rules can change from time to time. For example, while child custody may be the assigned task of the mediator, the program may not permit the discussion to also include property or support issues. If you have any questions about what is and is not appropriate for mediation, ask your lawyer.

7.2 How are mediation and negotiation different from a *collaborative divorce*?

Collaborative law is a method of resolving a divorce case where both parties have expressed a strong commitment to settling their disputes and avoiding litigation. You and your spouse each hire an attorney trained in the collaborative law process. The parties and lawyers enter into an agreement that provides that in the event either you or your spouse decides to take the case to court, both of you must terminate services with your collaborative lawyers and start all over again with new lawyers.

Often, spouses in the collaborative process enlist the support of other professionals, such as an independent financial advisor or coaches, to support them and answer questions through the process. While the process may be lengthy, it tries to shift the focus away from the conflict and toward finding solutions. The attorneys become a part of the team supporting settlement rather than advocates for one side's position, which can be seen as adding to the conflict.

Practitioners and academic reviewers are divided on the question of whether the collaborative divorce process is really easier, less expensive, or better than traditional representation and litigation. Talk to your lawyer about whether your case would be well suited to the collaborative law process.

7.3 What is involved in the mediation process? What will I have to do and how long will it take?

The mediation process will be explained to you in detail by the mediator at the start of the mediation session. Mediation involves one or more meetings with you, your spouse, and the mediator. In some cases the attorneys will also be present.

The mediator will outline ground rules designed to ensure you will be treated respectfully and given an opportunity to be heard. In most cases, you and your spouse will each be given an opportunity to make some opening remarks about what is important to you in the outcome of your divorce.

How long the process of mediation continues depends upon many of the same factors that affect how long your divorce will take. These include how many issues you and your spouse disagree about, the complexity of these issues, and the willingness of each of you to work toward an agreement.

Your case could settle after just a couple of mediation sessions or it might require a series of meetings. It is common for the mediator to clarify at the close of each session whether the parties are willing to continue with another session.

7.4 My lawyer said that mediation and negotiation can reduce delays in completing my divorce. How can they do this?

When the issues in your divorce are decided by a judge instead of by you and your spouse, there are many opportunities for delay. These can include:

- Conducting formal discovery to get proof of matters that might simply be agreed to in negotiation or mediation
- Preparing for and waiting for the trial date
- Having to return to court on a later, second date if your trial is not completed on the day it is scheduled
- Waiting for the judge's ruling on your case
- Needing additional court hearings after your trial to resolve disputes about the intention of the judge's rulings, issues that were overlooked, or disagreement regarding the language of the decree

Each one of these events holds the possibility of delaying your divorce by days, weeks, or even months. Mediating or negotiating the terms of your divorce decree can eliminate these delays.

7.5 How can mediation and negotiation lower the costs of my divorce?

If your case is not settled by agreement, you will be going to trial. If the issues in your case are many or if they are difficult or complex, such as custody, the attorney's fees and other costs of going to trial can be substantial.

By settling your case without going to trial, you may be able to save thousands of dollars in legal fees. Ask your attorney for a litigation budget that sets forth the potential costs of going to trial, so that you have some idea of these costs when deciding whether to settle an issue or to take it to trial before the judge.

7.6 Are there other benefits to mediating or negotiating a settlement?

Yes. A divorce resolved by a mediated or negotiated agreement can have these additional benefits:

Recognizing Common Goals. Mediation and negotiation allow for brainstorming between the parties and lawyers. Looking at all possible solutions, even the impractical ones, invites creative solutions to common goals. For example, suppose you and your spouse both agree that you need to pay your spouse some amount of equity for the family home you will keep, but you have no cash to make the payment. Together, you might come up with a number of options for accomplishing that goal and select the best one. By contrast, a judge is much more likely to simply order you to pay the money without considering all of the possible options.

Addressing the Unique Circumstances of Your Situation. Rather than using a one-size-fits-all approach as a judge might do, a settlement reached by agreement allows you and your spouse to consider the unique circumstances of your situation in formulating a good outcome. For example, suppose you disagree about the parenting times for the Thanksgiving holiday. The judge might order you to alternate the holiday each year, even though you both would have preferred to have your child share the day.

Creating a Safe Place for Communication. Mediation and negotiation give each party an opportunity to be heard. Perhaps you and your spouse have not yet had an opportunity to share directly your concerns about settlement. For example, you might be worried about how the temporary parenting time arrangement is impacting your children, but have not yet talked to your spouse about it. A mediation session or settlement conference can be a safe place for you and your spouse to communicate your concerns about your children or your finances.

Fulfilling Your Children's Needs. You may see that your children would be better served by you and your spouse deciding their future rather than having it decided by a judge who does not know, love, and understand your children like the two of you do.

Eliminating the Risk and Uncertainty of Trial. If a judge decides the outcome of your divorce, you give up control over the terms of the settlement. The decisions are left in the hands of the judge. If you and your spouse reach agreement, however, you have the power to eliminate the risk of an uncertain outcome.

Reducing the Risk of Harm to Your Children. If your case goes to trial on the issue of child custody, it is likely that you and your spouse will give testimony that will be upsetting to one another. As conflict increases, the relationship between you and your spouse inevitably deteriorates. This can be harmful to your children, in both the short term and in future years. That result can be reduced, or avoided, if resolution is reached through negotiation or mediation, in which you seek to reach agreement regardless of the conflicts that led to the divorce in the first place. It is not unusual for the relationship between the parents to improve if the professionals succeed in creating a safe environment for rebuilding communication and reaching agreements in the best interests of a child.

Having the Support of Professionals. Using trained professionals such as mediators and lawyers to support you can help you to reach a settlement that you might think is impossible at the start of the divorce process. These professionals have skills that may help both parties get past anger and other emotions, shift attention away from irrelevant facts, and focus on what is actually most important to each party. They understand the law and know the possible outcomes if your case goes to trial.

Lowering Stress. The process of preparing for and going to court can be stressful, no matter how a trial comes out. Your energy is also going toward caring for your children, looking at your finances, and coping with the emotions of divorce. You might decide that you would be better served by settling your case rather than proceeding to trial.

Achieving Closure. When you are going through a divorce, the process can feel as though it is taking an eternity. By reaching agreement, you and your spouse are better able to put the divorce behind you and move forward with your lives.

7.7 Is mediation mandatory?

Sometimes. Mediation is not mandatory in Nevada in all cases. Depending upon the county in which your divorce is filed, if minor children are involved in the divorce, mediation may be required in most cases to develop a plan for matters related to the children, such as custody and parenting time. The rules change from time to time, and there are exceptions to the requirements even when such a requirement is applicable. Discuss with your attorney whether mediation will be required in your case.

7.8 What if I want to try mediation and my spouse doesn't?

Unless you live in a county in which mediation for child custody/visitation is mandatory, you can't force your spouse into mediation. As a general rule, it takes two willing parties to mediate successfully; there can be negative consequences in court for a party who is required to participate in mediation but refuses to do so.

7.9 My spouse abused me and I am afraid to participate in mediation. Should I participate anyway?

If you have been a victim of domestic violence by your spouse, it is important that you discuss the appropriateness of mediation with your attorney. Mediation may not be a safe way for you to reach agreement. If the court rule in your county requires mediation, talk to your attorney about whether seeking a waiver of mediation is an appropriate option.

Prior to allowing mediation to proceed, any mediator should ask you whether you have been a victim of domestic violence. This is critical for the mediator to both assess your safety and to ensure that the balance of power in the mediation process is maintained. The court mediation centers have special protocols for mediation they use when there has been a history of domestic violence.

Whether or not there is a documented history of domestic violence, if you feel threatened or intimidated by your spouse but still want to proceed with mediation, talk to your attorney about him or her attending the mediation sessions with you, or mediating with your spouse being in a separate room. For private mediation outside the court mediation centers, consider asking to have the mediation occur at your lawyer's office, where you feel more comfortable.

If you do participate in mediation, insist that your mediator have a good understanding of the dynamics of domestic abuse and how they can impact the mediation process.

7.10 What training and credentials do mediators have?

The background of mediators varies, and the availability of mediators varies depending upon where you live. If you live in or near either Las Vegas or Reno, you will find many competent mediators. However, if you live in a rural county, mediators may not be available to you.

Some mediators are attorneys; many come from other backgrounds such as counseling. Some mediators have received their training through the continuing legal education through one of the state's bar associations. Ask your attorney for help in finding a qualified mediator who is competent in mediating family law cases.

7.11 What types of issues can be mediated or negotiated?

All of the issues in your case *can* be mediated or negotiated. However, in advance of any mediation or negotiation session, you should discuss with your lawyer which issues you want to be mediated or negotiated, or what subjects are or are not on the agenda to be discussed.

The local court rules in your county may require that you participate in mediation of matters concerning your children, at least as to custody. Sometimes, that mediation expressly does not include consideration of child support.

The ethical rules governing lawyers and litigants—and common sense about looking out for children—state that child custody should be addressed with the sole intention of looking out for the best interest of the children, and child custody should never be contested for either financial leverage or vindictiveness.

Even so, it is necessary for you to understand the impact of the decisions that you make. Talk with your lawyer in advance of any mediation about custody to be absolutely clear about the impact of custody decisions on child support, possible future relocation motions, and perhaps other issues, such as occupancy of the former marital home. Custody terms can drastically alter both child support and some property issues, and you should understand those impacts before you negotiate child custody and parenting time.

You may decide that certain issues are nonnegotiable for you. Discuss this with your attorney in advance of any mediation or negotiation sessions so that he or she can advise whether your expectations are legally supportable and, if so, assist you in focusing the discussions on the issues you are open to looking at.

7.12 What is the role of my attorney in the mediation process?

The role of your attorney in the mediation process will vary depending upon your situation. In pretty much every mediation, however, you should confer with your attorney in advance of attending mediation about what to expect, how the process works, and in formulating your goals and intentions. While the process is one of discussion, you should be as clear as possible as to what you want in advance of attending, and should have advice as to whether your expectations are legally realistic. Your attorney can assist you in identifying which issues should be discussed in mediation and which are better left to negotiations or resolution in court.

As discussed above, you should know in advance how various physical custody orders can affect child support and other issues. In all cases, it is important that your attorney review any agreements discussed in mediation before a final agreement is reached. There is nothing wrong with stating that before you sign an agreement, you want to have your lawyer review it with you. A mediator should never tell you not to discuss things with your lawyer.

7.13 How do I prepare for mediation?

Prior to attending a mediation session with your spouse, discuss with your attorney the issues you intend to mediate. In particular, be sure to discuss the impact of custody and parenting time arrangements on child support. Enlist your attorney's support in identifying your intentions for the mediation.

Writing an outline or listing major points is often useful. Make a list of the issues important to you. For example, when it comes to your child, you might consider whether it is your child's safety, the parenting time schedule, or the ability to attend your children's events that concerns you most.

Be forward looking. Giving thought to your desired outcomes while approaching mediation with an open mind and heart is the best way to move closer to settlement.

7.14 Do children attend the mediation sessions?

In most cases your child will not participate in mediation. However, your case might be an exception if you have an older child who is sufficiently mature to participate in the process in one way or another.

If you think your child should be involved, talk to your lawyer and your mediator about the potential risks and benefits of including the child in the process. Sometimes, alternatives to having the child participate in the mediation session include an interview or statement to a third party.

7.15 I want my attorney to look over the agreements my spouse and I discussed in mediation before I give my final approval. Is this possible?

Yes. Before giving your written or final approval to any agreements reached in mediation, it is wise that your attorney review those agreements with you. This is necessary to ensure that you understand the terms of the settlement and its implications, including the impact of the agreement on other aspects of your case that may not have been discussed during mediation. Your attorney will also review the agreement for compliance with Nevada law.

7.16 Who pays for mediation?

It depends. The cost of mediation usually must be paid for by you or your spouse, or both. Often, it is a shared expense; sometimes, the court directs who pays how much of the cost of mediation.

The court-provided mediation programs usually operate on a sliding scale depending on the income of the parties. Expect your mediator to address the matter of fees before or at your first session.

7.17 What if mediation fails?

If mediation is not successful, you still may be able to settle your case through negotiations between the attorneys. Also, partial agreements are possible—you and your spouse can agree to preserve the settlements that were reached and to take only the remaining disputed issues to the judge for trial.

7.18 What is a *settlement conference*?

A *settlement conference* is usually a meeting between you, your lawyer, your spouse, and your spouse's lawyer, with the intention of negotiating the terms of your divorce. Typically, no mediator or other third party is present, but in some cases, a professional with important information needed to support the settlement process, such as an accountant, may also participate. Anything both sides agree to can be arranged.

A settlement conference can be a powerful tool for the resolution of your case. Settlement conferences are most effective when both parties and their attorneys see the potential for a negotiated resolution and have the necessary information to accomplish that goal.

7.19 Why should I consider a settlement conference when the attorneys can negotiate through letters and phone calls?

A settlement conference can eliminate the delays that often occur when negotiation takes place through correspondence and calls between the attorneys. Rather than waiting days or weeks for a response—which may or may not be based on a full understanding of what was offered—you can receive a response on a proposal in a matter of minutes, and clarify any misunderstandings on the spot.

A settlement conference also enables you and your spouse, if you choose, to use your own words to explain the reasoning behind your requests. You are also able to provide information immediately to expedite the process.

7.20 How do I prepare for my settlement conference?

Being well prepared for the settlement conference can help you make the most of this opportunity to resolve your case without the need to go to trial. Actions you should take include:

- Provide in advance of the conference all necessary information. If your attorney has asked you for a current pay stub, tax return, debt amounts, asset values, or other documentation, make sure it is provided prior to the meeting.
- Discuss your topics of concern with your attorney in advance. Your lawyer will need to know what you want in order to ensure all such matters are addressed in the discussion. Your lawyer can also assist you in understanding your rights under the law so that you can have realistic expectations for the outcome of negotiations.
- Bring a positive attitude, a listening ear, and an open mind. Come with the attitude that your case will settle. Be willing to first listen to the opposing party, and then to share your response and position. This will encourage your spouse to listen to your position before responding. Resist the urge to interrupt.

Few cases settle without each side demonstrating flexibility and a willingness to compromise. Most cases settle when the parties are able to bring these qualities and attitudes to the process.

7.21 What will happen at my settlement conference?

Typically, the conference will be held at the office of one of the attorneys, with both parties and lawyers present. If there are a number of issues to be discussed, an agenda may be used to keep the focus on relevant topics. From time to time throughout the conference, you and your attorney may meet alone to consult as needed. If additional information is needed to reach agreement, some issues may be set aside for later discussion.

The length of the conference depends upon the number of issues to be resolved, the complexity of the issues, and the willingness of the parties and lawyers to communicate effectively. An effort is usually made to confirm which issues have been previously resolved and which issues remain disputed. Then, one by one, the remaining issues are addressed.

7.22 What is the role of my attorney in the settlement conference?

Your attorney is your advocate during the settlement conference. You can count on him or her to support you throughout the process, to see that important issues are addressed, and to counsel you privately outside of the presence of your spouse and his or her lawyer.

7.23 Why is my lawyer appearing so friendly with my spouse and her lawyer?

Successful negotiations rely upon building trust between the parties working toward agreement. Your lawyer may be respectful or pleasant toward your spouse or your spouse's lawyer to promote a good outcome for you.

It is nearly always in the best interest of both parties if the attorneys get along with one another well enough to facilitate the discussion between them and between the parties. Any extra time consumed in dealing with emotions by the lawyers is at the expense of the parties.

Additionally, remember that your lawyer is a professional who may have an ongoing professional relationship with the other attorney. Rarely do your issues warrant the destruction of a working professional relationship with the other attorney.

7.24 What happens if my spouse and I settled some but not all of the issues in our divorce?

You and your spouse can agree to maintain the agreements you have reached and let the judge decide those matters that you are unable to resolve.

7.25 If my spouse and I reach an agreement, how long will it take before we can go before the judge to have it approved at a final hearing?

Often, if the attorneys report to the court that an agreement has been reached, the court will schedule a "prove up hearing" within days to allow the agreement to be put on the record in open court, with the parties being asked to confirm that what is spoken is their agreement. One of the lawyers then prepares formal paperwork spelling out the terms in writing, and submits it for filing.

In other cases, the agreement is put in writing and submitted to the court "on the papers" without any hearing, to be signed and filed by the court.

In most cases, if a settlement is reached through negotiation or mediation, the case can be concluded, one way or the other, within thirty days or so.

8

Emergency: When You Fear Your Spouse

Suddenly you are in a panic. Maybe your spouse was serious when threatening to take your child and leave the state. What if you're kicked out of your own home? Suppose all of the bank accounts are emptied? Your fear heightens as your mind spins with every horror story you've ever heard about divorce.

Facing an emergency situation in divorce can feel as though your entire life is at stake. You may not be able to concentrate on anything else. At the same time, you may be paralyzed with anxiety and have no idea how to begin to protect yourself. You have countless worries about what your future holds.

Remember that you have overcome many challenges in your life before this moment. There are people willing to help you. You have strength and wisdom you may not yet even realize. Step by step, you will make it through again this time.

When facing an emergency, do your best to focus on what to do in the immediate moment. Set aside your worries about the future for another day. Now it is time to stay in the present moment, let others support you, and start taking action right away.

8.1 My spouse has deserted me, and I need to get divorced as quickly as possible. What is my first step??

Your first step is to get legal advice as soon as possible. The earlier you get legal counsel to advise you about your rights, and what actions actually need to be taken in what order, the better. The initial consultation will answer most of your questions and start you on an action plan for getting your divorce underway.

8.2 I'm afraid my abusive spouse will try to hurt me and/ or our children if I say I want a divorce. What can I do legally to protect myself and my children?

Develop a plan with your safety and that of your children as your highest priority. In addition to meeting with an attorney at your first opportunity, develop a safety plan in the event you and your children need to escape your home.

A great way to do this is to let in support from an agency that helps victims of domestic violence. Call the National Domestic Violence Hotline at (800) 799-7233, or contact the Nevada Network Against Domestic Violence, 220 S. Rock Blvd., Suite 116, Reno, NV 89502 2355, at (775) 828-1115; (800) 500-1556 (in State); fax: (775) 828-9911; website: www.nnadv.org, to get more information about the domestic violence program closest to you.

At least in the larger communities in Nevada, there are local domestic violence shelters, which have trained staff who can help. In Clark County, consider Safe Nest, at (702) 646-4981; (800) 486-7282) (rural) or Safe House, at (702) 564-3227. Both agencies' hotlines are answered twenty-four hours a day. The United Way of Northern Nevada and the Sierra, at (775) 333-8287, maintains a list of Northern Nevada shelters and agencies.

Background information, referral information, and the relevant statutes concerning domestic violence and protection orders are posted and explained at http://willicklawgroup.com/domestic-violence/.

Your risk of harm from an abusive spouse increases when you leave. For this reason, all actions must be taken with safety as the first concern.

Find a lawyer who understands domestic violence. Often, your local domestic violence agency can help with a referral. Talk to your lawyer about the concerns for your safety and that of your children. Ask your lawyer about a *protection order,* sometimes called a *TPO (temporary protection order)* or *TRO (temporary restraining order).* This is a court order that may offer a number of protections including granting you temporary custody of your children for a limited period, ordering your spouse to leave the family residence and have no contact with you, and ordering temporary support.

8.3 I am afraid to meet with a lawyer because I am terrified my spouse will find out and get violent. What should I do?

Schedule an initial consultation with an attorney who is experienced in working with domestic violence victims. When you schedule the appointment, let the firm know your situation and instruct the law office not to place any calls to you which you think your spouse might discover. If you think your calls or e-mails are being monitored, make the call or contact from someone else's phone or computer.

Consultations with your attorney are confidential. Your lawyer has an ethical duty to not disclose your meeting with anyone outside of the law firm. Let your attorney know your concerns so that extra precautions can be taken by the law office in handling your file.

8.4 I want to give my attorney all the information needed so my children and I are safe from my spouse. What does this include?

Provide your attorney with complete information about the history, background, and nature of your abuse, noting any evidence that exists such as:

- The types of abuse (for example, physical, sexual, verbal, financial, mental, emotional)
- The dates, time frames, or occasions
- The locations
- Whether you were ever treated medically, and if any records of that treatment exist
- Any police reports made
- E-mails, letters, notes, or journal entries
- Any photographs taken
- Any witnesses or evidence of the abuse

- Any statements made by your spouse admitting the abuse
- Any known abuse of others—former spouses, children, or pets
- Alcohol or drug abuse by your spouse
- The possession of guns or other weapons by your spouse

The better the information you provide to your lawyer, the easier it will be for him or her to make a strong case for the protection of you and your children.

8.5 I'm not ready to hire a lawyer for a divorce, but I am afraid my spouse is going to get violent with my children and me in the meantime. What can I do?

It is possible to seek a protection order from the court without an attorney, and without filing for divorce. It is possible for the judge to order your spouse out of your home, granting you custody of your children for a limited time, ordering your spouse to stay away from you, and providing for temporary support. Depending on the circumstances, these orders can be extended for up to a year.

8.6 What's the difference between a *protection order* and a *restraining order*?

Procedures, and the names of orders, are different from place to place, and have changed over time. *Protection orders* and *restraining orders* are both court orders directing a person to not engage in certain behavior. Both of these orders are intended to protect others. While either order can initially be obtained without notice to the other person, that person always has a right to a hearing to determine whether a protection order or restraining order should remain in place.

Practice and procedure varies from county to county. In most jurisdictions a temporary protective order against domestic violence can be obtained if there is a "domestic relationship" between the applicant and the adverse party (the party against whom the order is entered) and is provided free at family court (in jurisdictions with a family court).

A protective order issued by justice court can be against stalking and harassment, harm to minors, sexual assault, or harassment in the workplace (these are to be filed by the owner or the agent of the business).

Justice court protective orders may incur a fee. Typically, no fees are assessed when an individual files for an order, but if the case goes to a hearing, the judge has discretion to impose the full filing fee, a reduced fee, or no fee against the adverse party. If the case does not proceed to a hearing before a judge, fees are generally considered "deferred" indefinitely. A fee is charged for filing an application against harassment in the workplace.

Talk to your attorney about obtaining a protection order if you are concerned about the safety of your children or yourself or if there has been a history of domestic violence. The violation of a protection order is a criminal offense which can result in immediate arrest.

If you are concerned that your spouse will annoy, threaten, harass, or intimidate you after your divorce complaint is filed, ask your lawyer about a restraining order. If your spouse violates the restraining order, he or she may be brought before the court for contempt.

8.7 My spouse has never been violent, but is going to be really angry and upset when the divorce papers are served. Do I need a protection order?

The facts of your case may not warrant a protection order. However, if you are concerned about your spouse's behavior, there are a few other steps you can consider.

Ask your attorney about the *joint preliminary injunction (JPI)* to be delivered to your spouse at the same time as the divorce complaint. This injunction not only prohibits marital property from being disposed of, it also directs your spouse not to annoy, threaten, intimidate, or harass you while the divorce is in progress. Remember, this is a joint injunction, meaning that it applies to you as well.

If you are concerned that things may "go missing" or be destroyed, consider taking a photo inventory of the premises, and securing any property that might disappear, before serving the divorce complaint.

Consider how you wish to have the complaint served. Sometimes, a lawyer makes a phone call and invites a person to accept service and sign a receipt rather than being served, which might be less provoking. If service is to be made, consider where and when you want this to be accomplished, and whether you want to be sure you are not there at the time.

8.8 How will a temporary protection order (TPO) protect me from physical harm at the hands of my spouse? What will happen if my spouse violates the TPO?

The reality is that a *temporary protection order (TPO)* is a piece of paper. It is still up to you to be prudent about looking after your own physical safety. What the TPO gives you is a court record so if your spouse shows up where he or she is not supposed to be, or threatens or assaults you, you have a way of bringing your spouse before a judge to answer for his or her actions. If you have a TPO in place and the police are called, it is much easier for them to determine what is going on and make the correct decision as to what to do about it.

The range of penalties for violation of a TPO include monetary damages and possible incarceration (being put in jail) for violation of the order.

8.9 My spouse says that I am crazy, that I am a liar, and that no judge will ever believe me if I tell the truth about the abusive behavior. What can I do if I don't have any proof?

Most domestic violence is not witnessed by third parties. Often, there is little physical evidence. Judges, of course, know this.

Even without physical evidence, such as pictures or police reports, a judge can enter orders to protect you and your children if you give truthful testimony about your abuse which the judge finds believable. Your own testimony of your abuse is evidence.

It is very common for persons who abuse others to claim that their victims are liars and to make statements intended to discourage disclosure of the abuse. This is just another form of controlling behavior.

Your attorney's skills and experience will support you to give effective testimony in the courtroom to establish your case. Let your lawyer know your concerns so that a strong case can be presented to the judge based upon your persuasive statements of the truth of your experience.

8.10 I'm afraid my spouse is going to take all of the money out of the bank accounts and leave me with nothing. What can I do?

Talk to your attorney immediately. If you are worried about your spouse emptying financial accounts or selling marital assets, it is critical that you take action at once. Your attorney can advise you on your right to take possession of certain assets in order to protect them from being hidden or spent by your spouse, or to take other steps, using credit or other means, to be sure you are not left destitute before you can get to court.

Ask your lawyer about seeking a joint preliminary injunction (JPI). As explained in question 8.7, this injunction forbids either of you from selling, transferring, hiding, or otherwise disposing of marital property until the divorce is complete.

A JPI is intended to prevent assets from "disappearing" before a final division of the property from your marriage is complete. Violations of the JPI can be addressed in court, and can result in sanctions, compensation to the innocent spouse, and contempt findings against the violating party. A party violating a TPO can be ordered to "make the other party whole"—in other words, repay the other party for all money lost because of violation of the TPO.

If you're concerned that your spouse may empty financial accounts, talk to your lawyer about the benefits of obtaining a JPI as to property before giving your spouse notice that you are filing for divorce, or taking other steps.

8.11 My spouse told me that if I ever file for divorce, I'll never see my child again. Should I be worried about my child being abducted?

Your fear that your spouse will abduct your child is a common one. While most such threats are empty, it is serious enough that while you should not panic, you should seriously consider some of the factors that appear to increase the risk that your child will be removed from the state by the other parent.

Risk factors include:

- Any history of prior abductions, attempted abductions, or threatened abductions
- Abandoning employment
- Selling a primary residence, or terminating a lease
- Closing bank accounts, liquidating assets, or hiding or destroying documents
- Applying for a passport or visa, or obtaining travel documents for the child or other person
- Seeking the child's school or medical records
- Any history of domestic violence, stalking, or child abuse or neglect
- Prior refusal to obey child-custody or visitation orders
- An absence of strong family, emotional, or cultural ties to this state
- Strong ties to some other state or country, particularly one that does not have laws requiring the return of kidnaped children
- Immigration or citizenship status difficulties of your spouse that might make it difficult to remain in the United States legally
- Your spouse has had an application for U.S. citizenship denied
- Your spouse has ever used forged or misleading documents to obtain a passport, visa, driver's license, etc
- Your spouse has used multiple names in an effort mislead or commit fraud

The risk of child abduction appears more serious in relationships between parties that cross culture, race, religion, or ethnicity. A lower socioeconomic status, or prior criminal record, also appear to be related to abduction risk. Programming and brainwashing are often present in cases where a child is at risk for being kidnaped by a parent, and efforts to isolate the child may also be seen.

Nevada has special laws designed to prevent child abduction by preventing the child's travel or removal from school, by imposing supervised visitation, or doing whatever is necessary. For background information and a discussion of these laws, see the materials posted at http://willicklawgroup.com/child-abduction-kidnaping-and-recovery/. Ensure that your lawyer is familiar with these laws.

Talk to your lawyer to assess the risks in your particular case. Together you can determine whether statements by your spouse are threats intended to control or intimidate you or whether legal action is needed to protect your child.

8.12 What legal steps can be taken to prevent my spouse from removing our child from the state?

If you are concerned about your child being removed from the state, ask your lawyer whether any of these options might be available in your case:

- A court order giving you immediate custody until a temporary custody hearing can be held
- A court order directing your spouse to turn over passports for the child and your spouse to the court
- The posting of a bond prior to your spouse exercising parenting time
- Supervised visitation by your spouse
- Imposition of travel restrictions relating to the child
- A requirement to obtain orders or guarantees from the officials of other countries before visitation with the child is permitted
- Issuing a warrant to take physical custody of the child
- Directing law enforcement assistance

Both state and federal laws are designed to provide protection from the removal of children from one state to another when a custody matter is brought and to protect children from kidnaping. *The Uniform Child Custody Jurisdiction Enforcement Act (UCCJEA)* was passed to encourage the custody of children to generally be decided in the state where they have been living most recently and where they have the most ties. There are criminal laws, both state and federal, designed to deter and punish kidnaping as well. For a description of some of those laws and how they apply, see http://willicklawgroup.com/child-abduction-kidnaping-and-recovery/.

If you are concerned about your child being abducted, talk with your lawyer about all options available to you for your child's protection.

8.13 What happens if my spouse removes our child from Nevada anyway?

If your spouse removes your child from Nevada despite a court order prohibiting it, immediately consult your attorney. Depending on the facts, a warrant to take the child into protective custody, or for arrest of your spouse, or both, can be ordered.

The rules governing interstate remedies for abduction are complicated. Some background is set out at http://willicklaw-group.com/child abduction kidnaping and recovery/. The short version, however, is that you can bring law enforcement into play to help recover your child.

8.16 If there is an incident or conflict with my spouse, will I be ordered out of my home?

You or your spouse could file a motion for *exclusive possession* of the home, seeking to have the other spouse ordered to move out of the house.

Abusive behavior is one basis for seeking temporary possession of the home. If there are minor children, the custodial parent will ordinarily be awarded temporary possession of the residence, so that the children do not have to relocate. Other factors the judge may consider include:

- Whether one of you owned the home prior to the marriage
- After provisions are made for payment of temporary support, who can afford to remain in the home or obtain other housing
- Who is most likely to be awarded the home in the divorce

- Options available to each of you for other temporary housing, including other homes, friends, or family members who live in the area
- Special needs that would make a move unduly burdensome, such as a health condition or special accommodations in the home
- Self-employment operating out of the home, which could not be readily moved, such as a child-care business

If staying in the home is important to you, talk to your attorney about your reasons so that a strong case can be made for you at the hearing.

9

Child Custody

Ever since you and your spouse began talking about divorce, chances are your children have been your greatest concern. You or your spouse might have postponed the decision to seek divorce because of concern about the impact on your children. Now that the time has come, you might still have doubts about whether your children will be all right after the divorce.

Remember that you have been doing your best to make wise and loving decisions for your children since they were born. You've always tried to see that they had everything they really needed. You've loved them and protected them. This won't change simply because you are going through a divorce. You worked to be a good parent before the divorce and you will be a good parent after the divorce.

It can be difficult not to worry about how the sharing of parenting time with your spouse will affect your children. You may also have fears about being cut out of your child's life. Try to remember that, regardless of who has primary custody, it is likely that the court order will not only give you a lot of time with your children but also a generous opportunity to be involved in their day-to-day lives.

With the help of your lawyer, you can make sound decisions regarding the custody arrangement that is in the best interest of your children.

9.1 What types of custody are awarded in Nevada?

Under Nevada law, there are two aspects to a custody determination. These are legal custody and physical custody.

Legal custody refers to the power to make important decisions regarding your children. The Nevada Supreme Court has defined it as "having basic legal responsibility for a child and making major decisions regarding the child, including the child's health, education, and religious upbringing."

Legal custody may be awarded to you, to your spouse, or to both of you jointly. In Nevada, joint legal custody is the norm. A parent is rarely divested of legal custodial rights unless there is a severe—usually criminal—issue that has arisen concerning that parent.

If you have *sole legal custody,* you are the primary and final decision maker for significant matters regarding your children, such as which school they attend and who their health care providers are. The noncustodial parent likely still has parenting time and other rights, but does not have the right to make those decisions.

Joint legal custody means that you and your former spouse share equally in the decision making for your child. If you and the other parent are unable to reach agreement, you may need to return to mediation or to court for the decision to be made.

Joint legal custody requires the following:

- Effective and open communication between the parents concerning the child
- A strong desire on the part of both parents to continue to co-parent together
- A willingness to accept differing parenting values
- A willingness on the part of both parents to place the child's needs before their own
- Both parents' willingness to be flexible and compromising about making decisions concerning the child

Physical custody refers to the physical location of the children, that is, where they spend their time. Like legal custody, it may be awarded to one parent solely, or to both parents jointly. It also may be awarded primarily to one parent, and secondarily to the other.

In 2009, the Nevada Supreme Court stated that any time-sharing between parents in which each parent has at least 40 percent of the time with the child, constitutes "joint custody" under Nevada law. That works out, roughly, to a time share of four days a week with one parent, and three days with the other.

If there is more than one child and one of your children will reside with you while another child will reside with the other parent, the arrangement is referred to as *split physical custody.*

Specific parenting time must be clearly stated in any parenting agreement, regardless of who has physical custody. Provisions for days of the week, school breaks, summer and other vacations, and holidays are typically made in detail.

Be sure to discuss with your attorney not only the best interest of your child, but also the possible effects of all possible custody arrangements on every other issue involved in your divorce. Your attorney should be able to quickly advise how any proposed custodial arrangement will affect the other issues.

9.2 On what basis will the judge award custody?

The judge considers many factors in determining child custody. Most important is "the best interest of the child." To determine best interest, the judge may look at the factors described below, which are required to be considered by the statute governing how a court may award child custody:

- The wishes of the child if the child is of sufficient age and capacity to form an intelligent preference as to his or her custody
- Any nomination by a parent of a guardian for the child
- Which parent is more likely to allow the child to have frequent associations and a continuing relationship with the noncustodial parent
- The level of conflict between the parents
- The ability of the parents to cooperate to meet the needs of the child
- The mental and physical health of the parents

- The physical, developmental, and emotional needs of the child
- The nature of the relationship of the child with each parent
- The ability of the child to maintain a relationship with any sibling
- Any history of parental abuse or neglect of the child or a sibling of the child
- Whether either parent or any other person seeking custody has engaged in an act of domestic violence against the child, a parent of the child, or any other person residing with the child

Generally, it is common for the court to consider a wide range of facts and assertions about the parents and their respective capacities to care for children. Terms that might be used in the arguments by the lawyers or decision by the court not specifically set out in the above list include:

Home Environment. This refers to the physical, financial, emotional, and cultural environments offered by you and your spouse. The court may consider factors such as the safety, stability, and nurturing found in each home.

Emotional Ties. The emotional relationship between the child and each parent may include the nature of the bond between the parent and child and the feelings shared between the child and each parent.

Continuity of Care. If one parent stayed at home for a period of years or otherwise provided the majority of actual care of a child, some judges consider that an award of custody altering that situation could disrupt the well-being of the child.

Domestic Violence or Prior Parental Kidnaping. Both domestic violence and any history of parental kidnaping are called out by the statutes as creating a presumption that the person doing such acts should not get either sole or joint custody of a child. The presumption can be overcome, but any such history makes obtaining such an award much more difficult. If either domestic violence or parental kidnaping—on either side—is a concern in your case, be sure to discuss it in detail with your attorney during the initial consultation so that every measure can be taken to protect the safety of you and your children.

There are a number of myths or urban legends about custody that continue to exist, even though they do not apply in modern Nevada custody law.

For example, Nevada no longer ascribes to the "tender years" doctrine, which formerly gave a preference for custody of very young children to the mother.

Similarly, while the extent to which a judge assesses the morals of a parent can vary greatly from judge to judge, sexual conduct will ordinarily not be considered unless your child was exposed to conduct actually harming the child. Simply claiming that your former spouse has an intimate relationship with someone is not usually relevant to the custody decision unless the person involved poses some danger of harm to the child.

Nevada, unlike some other states, does not allow a child to choose the parent with whom the child wishes to live. Rather, the court may consider the well-reasoned preferences of a child, at any age. Typically, the older the child, the greater the weight given to the preference. However, the child's reasoning is also important—judges will be alert to a child who expresses a preference for the more lenient parent, or for the parent who promises rewards or presents for the child's expressing a custody preference.

9.3 What's the difference between *visitation, parenting time,* and *custodial time*?

Historically, time spent with the noncustodial parent was referred to as *visitation*. Today, the term is disfavored by some, and courts tend to use terms like *parenting time* or *custodial time* for the time a child spends with either parent.

This change in language reflects the intention that children spend time with both parents and have two homes, as opposed to their living with one parent and "visiting" the other. The roles, and responsibilities, of parent and child are the same no matter the precise time share of either parent with the child.

9.4 How can I make sure I will get to keep the children during the divorce proceedings?

A temporary court order is the best way to be sure your children will stay with you while your divorce is proceeding. Even if you and your spouse have agreed to temporary arrangements, talk with your attorney about whether this agreement should be formalized in a court order so that it can be enforced.

Obtaining a temporary order can be an important protection not only for the custody of your children, but also for other issues such as support and temporary exclusive possession of the marital home.

Until a temporary order is entered, it's best that you continue to reside with your children if obtaining custody of them is important to you. It is usually recommended that the children stay in the family home. If you must leave your home, consider taking your children with you and talk with your attorney about seeking the appropriate court orders. These might include orders for temporary protection, custody, support, possession of your home, or attorney's fees.

However, do not allow a dispute on who leaves the house, or whether the children go along, to turn into an altercation. No court should look badly on a parent who avoided a conflict with the other and promptly sought to deal with the matter through the legal system rather than creating a scene in front of the children that could traumatize them. Leaving the house and promptly consulting a lawyer is not abandonment—it is often common sense.

9.5 How much weight does the child's preference carry?

As detailed above, the preference of your child is only one of many factors a judge considers in determining custody. Although there is no age at which your child's preference determines custody, most judges give more weight to the wishes of an older child.

The reasoning underlying your child's preference is also a factor to consider. Consider the fifteen-year-old girl who wants to live with her mother because "Mom lets me stay out past curfew, I get a bigger allowance, and I don't have to do chores." Greater weight might be given to the preference of an eight-year-old who wants to live with his mother because "she helps me with my homework, reads me bedtime stories, and doesn't call me names like Dad does."

If you see that your child's preference may be a factor in the determination of custody, discuss it with your lawyer so that this consideration is a part of assessing the action to be taken in your case.

9.6 How can I prove that I was the primary care provider?

One tool to assist you and your attorney in establishing your case as a primary care provider going forward, especially for younger children, is a chart indicating the care you and your spouse have each provided for your child. The clearer you are about the history of parenting, the better job your attorney can do in presenting your case to the judge.

Look at the activities in the chart to help you review the role of you and your spouse as care providers for your child.

Parental Roles Chart

Activity	Mother	Father
Attended prenatal medical visits	______	______
Attended prenatal class, if any	______	______
Took time off work after child was born	______	______
Got up with child for feedings	______	______
Regularly gets up with child in the morning	______	______
Regularly helped child get dressed in the morning	______	______
Stayed up with child when sick at night	______	______
Bathed child	______	______
Put child to sleep	______	______
Potty-trained child	______	______
Prepared and fed meals to child	______	______
Prepared school lunches for child	______	______
Helped child learn numbers, letters, colors, etc.	______	______
Helped child with practice for music, dance lessons, sports	______	______
Took time off work for child's appointments	______	______
Stayed home from work with sick child	______	______
Went to pharmacy for child's medication	______	______
Administered child's medication	______	______
Took child to therapy	______	______

Parental Roles Chart (Continued)

Activity	Mother	Father
Took child to doctor visits	______	______
Took child to optometrist	______	______
Took child to dentist	______	______
Took child to get haircuts	______	______
Bought clothing for child	______	______
Bought school supplies for child	______	______
Transported child to school	______	______
Picked up child after school	______	______
Drove carpool for child's school	______	______
Went to child's school activities	______	______
Helped child with homework and projects	______	______
Attended parent-teacher conferences	______	______
Helped in child's classroom	______	______
Chaperoned child's school trips and activities	______	______
Transported child to day care	______	______
Communicated with day care providers	______	______
Transported child from day care	______	______
Attended day care activities	______	______
Signed child up for sports, dance, music, etc.	______	______
Bought equipment for sports, dance, music	______	______
Regularly transported child to sports, dance, music	______	______
Attended sports, music, dance recitals	______	______
Coached child's sports, acted as Scout master, etc.	______	______
Transported child from sports, dance, music	______	______
Supervised the child's household chores	______	______
Supervised the child's TV watching, computer use, etc.	______	______
Knows child's friends and friend's families	______	______
Arranged for get-togethers with child's friends, sleepovers	______	______
Took child to religious education	______	______
Participated in child's religious education	______	______
Obtained information and training about special needs of child	______	______
Comforted child during times of emotional upset	______	______
Talked to child about child's problems (does the child turn to one parent more than the other?)	______	______

The court is required to look back over the past year to make a determination of what has actually happened in determining child custody.

If the answers to the questions from the parental role chart indicate that one parent has always done far more of such activities with and for the child than the other, their historical roles as actual child-care providers are established. If the parents disagree as to who did what, the disputed issue needs to be resolved.

Different judges will give different weight to the history of parental involvement with the child when deciding how child-care responsibilities should be shared after the divorce, but being clear about the history may give you, and your lawyer, a good idea of how to present your case.

9.7 Do I have to let my spouse see the children before we are actually divorced?

Unless your children are at risk for being harmed by your spouse, your child should normally maintain regular contact with the other parent.

It is important for children to experience the presence of both parents in their lives, regardless of the separation of the parents. Even if there is no temporary order for parenting time, cooperate with your spouse in making reasonable arrangements for both of you to have time with your child.

When safety is not an issue, if you deny contact with the other parent prior to trial, the judge is likely to question whether you have the best interest of your child at heart. Talk to your spouse or your lawyer about what parenting time schedule would be best for your child on a temporary basis.

9.8 I am seeing a therapist. Will that hurt my chances of getting custody?

If you are seeing a therapist, acknowledge yourself for getting the professional support you need. Your well being is important to enable you to be the best parent you can be.

Talk over with your lawyer the implications of your being treated by a therapist. It may be that the condition for which you are being treated in no way affects your child or your ability to be a loving and supportive parent. It may be that your history of actively addressing whatever issues are involved is the single best thing you could do for your position in court.

Your mental health records may be subpoenaed by the other parent's lawyer. For this reason it is important to discuss with your attorney an action plan for responding to a request to obtain records in your therapist's file. Ask your attorney to contact your therapist to alert him or her regarding how to respond to a request for your mental health records.

9.9 Can having a live-in partner hurt my chances of getting custody?

If you are contemplating having your partner live with you, discuss your decision with your attorney first. If you are already living with your partner, let your attorney know right away so that the potential impact on any custody ruling can be assessed.

Your living with someone who is not your spouse might have significant impact on your custody case. However, judges' opinions of the significance of this factor can vary greatly, and both social norms and legal standards have changed a great deal in recent years.

Talk promptly and frankly with your lawyer. It will be important for you to look together at many aspects, including the following:

- How the judge assigned to your case views this situation
- Whether your living arrangement is likely to prompt a custody dispute that would not otherwise arise
- How long have you been separated from the other parent
- How long you have been in a relationship with your new partner
- Whether anything in the makeup, history, or actions of your new partner present any issue or risk relating to the child
- The history and nature of the child's relationship with your new partner
- Your future plans with your new partner (such as marriage)

Living with a partner may—or may not—create issues for your custody case. Consider such a decision thoughtfully, taking into account the advice of your lawyer.

9.10 Will all the sordid details of my or my spouse's affair have to come out in court in front of our children?

Judges make every effort to protect children from the conflict of their parents. For this reason, most judges will not allow children to be present in the courtroom to hear the testimony of other witnesses, and court rules prohibit the parties from showing the papers or video record to the children.

While the risk that your spouse may share information with your child cannot be eliminated, it is not at all likely that a judge would even allow any of this testimony in the courtroom. Nevada is a no-fault divorce state—either party's accusations that the other is at fault, or has a moral failing, usually are irrelevant to any of the issues. Your or your spouse's affairs will have very little bearing on your case unless a claim for marital waste due to an affair, or some other damage claim, can be proven.

9.11 Should I hire a private detective to prove my spouse is having an affair?

Almost always, no. Again, unless significant community property has been wasted on third parties, or there are other issues such as transmission of diseases, the fact that an affair occurred or is ongoing usually has no bearing on the divorce case.

9.12 Will the fact that I had an affair during the marriage hurt my chances of getting custody?

For the most part, no. Only if it was found that your extramarital affair had some negative impact on the children should a judge consider the matter in a custody decision.

9.13 During the months it takes to get a divorce, is it okay to date or will it hurt my chances at custody?

Normally, it will make no difference. Nevada is a no-fault divorce state. Again, as long as you use discretion and do not negatively affect the children, your dating should not have any effect on your case.

9.14 Does my sexual orientation matter to my custody case?

There are no laws in Nevada that limit your rights as a parent based upon your sexual orientation. Social science research shows that gay and lesbian parents are more similar to than dissimilar from heterosexual parents, and the law is reaching the same conclusion, although the progress to that consensus has been uneven.

Exposing your child to sexual activity or engaging in sexual activity that harms your child are considered negative matters, and are therefore relevant factors in a custody dispute, regardless of sexual orientation. However, your sexual orientation is not the same as your sexual activity, and the question should always be the harm, if any, to the children, not the moral or religious beliefs of the other parent or the judge.

Be sure to choose a lawyer you are confident will fully support you in your goals as a parent. Understand that to dispel certain myths, stereotypes, or allegations, you may need to educate your spouse, opposing counsel, and the judge.

9.15 How is *abandonment* legally defined, and how might it affect the outcome of our custody battle?

Abandonment is rarely an issue in custody litigation unless one parent has been absent from the child's life for an extended period. Under Nevada law, abandonment is determined by the facts and circumstances of each case. Generally, it must have occurred for a period of six months or more and be without a just cause or excuse. The intentional absence of a parent's presence, care, protection, and support are all considered.

As a practical matter, this means that if you and your spouse separate, do not panic about being out of the house, or away from the children, for a short time if necessary. Of course, be sure the children are safe and are being cared for, but courts generally prefer to see parents avoid direct conflict and seek counsel rather than create a scene in front of the children.

Where abandonment has occurred for a period of six months or longer, a court may consider terminating parental rights, but only if doing so would be in the best interest of the child and not create an additional burden on the state welfare agencies. If you have any concern that such an allegation might be made, discuss it with your lawyer.

9.16 Can I have witnesses speak on my behalf to try to get custody of my children?

Absolutely. Witnesses are critical in every custody case. At a temporary custody hearing, a witness is more likely to provide testimony by affidavit or declaration, which is a written, sworn statement. However, at a trial for the final determination of custody, you and the other parent will normally each have an opportunity to have witnesses give live testimony on your behalf.

Among those you might consider as potential witnesses in your custody case are:

- Family members
- Family friends
- Child-care providers
- Neighbors
- Teachers
- Health care providers
- Clergy members

In considering which witnesses would best support your case, your attorney may consider the following:

- What has been this witness' opportunity to observe you or the other parent, especially with your child?
- How frequently? How recently?
- How long has the witness known you or the other parent?
- What is the relationship of the witness to the child and the parents?

- How valuable is the knowledge that this witness has?
- Does this witness have knowledge different from that of other witnesses?
- Is the witness available and willing to testify?
- Is the witness clear in conveying information?
- Is the witness credible, that is, will the judge believe this witness?
- Does the witness have any biases or prejudices that could negatively impact their testimony?

You and your attorney can work together to determine which witnesses will best support your case. Help your attorney by providing a list of potential witnesses together with your opinion regarding the answers to the above questions.

Give your attorney the phone numbers, addresses, and workplaces of each of your potential witnesses. This information can be critical to enabling the attorney to interview the witnesses, contact them regarding testifying, and issue subpoenas to compel their court attendance if needed. When parents give conflicting testimony during a custody trial, the testimony of other witnesses can be key to determining the outcome of the case.

9.17 How old do the children have to be before they can speak to the judge about with whom they want to live?

It depends upon the judge. There is no set age at which children are allowed to speak to the judge about their preferences as to custody.

If either you or your spouse wants the judge to listen to what your child has to say, a request is ordinarily made to the judge to have the child speak to the judge *in camera,* that is, in the judge's office (chambers) rather than from the witness stand.

Depending upon the judge's decision, the attorneys for you and your spouse may also be present. It is possible that the judge may allow the attorneys to question the child. If you have concerns about the other parent learning what your child says to the judge, talk to your lawyer about the possibility of obtaining a court order to keep this information from the other parent.

Some judges prefer children to simply be called to the witness stand in open court, like other witnesses. Even if taken *in camera,* typically the testimony of the child is made "on the record," that is, in the presence of a court reporter. This is so that the testimony can be transcribed later in the event of an appeal.

In addition to the age of a child, a judge may consider such facts as the child's maturity and personality in determining whether an *in camera* interview of the child by the judge, or regular in-court testimony, will be helpful to the custody decision-making process.

A judge may order an *outsourced evaluation* with either a psychologist or other mental health professional. In some places in Nevada, such as Clark County, the family mediation center arranges for child interviews by their staff mediators. The children's wishes are usually taken by the interviewer and presented to the judge in a written report. The cost of an evaluation or interview is usually split between the parties, but can be allocated differently by the judge.

9.18 Will my attorney want to speak with my children?

Usually not. As a practical matter, not all attorneys are trained in appropriate interviewing techniques for children, especially for younger children. If the attorney has not spent a lot of time with children or is not familiar with child development, the interview may not provide meaningful information and may actually cause damage.

The relevant ethical codes call for attorneys to generally "not initiate communication with the child, except in the presence of the child's lawyer or guardian *ad litem,* with court permission, or as necessary to verify facts in motions and pleadings." Contact between lawyers for the parties and the children at issue are disfavored by the relevant rules.

9.19 Who is a *guardian ad litem*? Why is one appointed?

In custody cases, a *guardian ad litem* is an individual who is sometimes appointed by the court to represent the best interests of the child. The guardian *ad litem* (sometimes referred to as the *GAL*), typically an attorney, is often directed by the judge to conduct an investigation on the issue of custody.

The guardian *ad litem* may be called as a witness by you or your spouse or by the judge to give testimony based upon the investigation. For example, the GAL might testify regarding the unsafe housing conditions of a parent. In some cases the attorneys may agree that a written report prepared by the guardian *ad litem* be received into evidence for the judge's consideration. In other cases, the GAL is directed by the judge to provide reports in writing, either on a set schedule or as the GAL determines to be necessary.

9.20 How might a video of my child help my custody case?

A video of your child's day-to-day life can help the judge learn more about your child's needs. It can demonstrate how your child interacts with you, siblings, and other important people in your family's life. The judge can see your child's room, home, and neighborhood.

Talk to your lawyer about whether a video—or other, similar, evidence—would be helpful in your case. Such a video should show routines in your child's day, including challenging moments such as bedtime or disciplining.

If your lawyer recommends making a video, talk with him or her about what scenes to include, the length of the video, keeping the original media, and the editing process.

Remember, a video may look staged. That would not work to your advantage, so making a video should be considered carefully before investing the time and effort.

9.21 Why might I not be awarded custody?

You will not be awarded custody if the judge determines that you are not fit to be a custodial parent. You may also not be awarded custody in the event the judge determines that, although you are fit to be awarded custody, it is in your child's best interest that custody is awarded to the other parent, or made joint.

Determinations of your fitness to be a custodial parent and of the best interest of your child will largely depend upon the facts of your case. Reasons why a parent might be found to be unfit include a history of physical abuse, alcohol or drug abuse, or mental health problems that affect the ability to parent. A judge's ruling on the best interest of a child is based upon numerous factors, which are discussed in detail above.

A decision by the judge that your spouse should have primary custody does not require a conclusion that you are an unfit parent. Even if the judge determines that both you and your spouse are fit to have custody, he or she may nevertheless decide that it is in the best interest of your child that only one of you be awarded custody.

9.22 Does joint custody always mean equal time at each parent's house?

No. Joint custody does not necessarily mean an equal division of parenting time, nor does it require that the child flip-flop every other week between two homes.

Joint custody in Nevada is defined as any schedule in which each parent has at least 40 percent of the custodial time with the child. Any less than that and the other parent is considered the primary custodian.

It can also be helpful to remember that day-to-day decisions, such as a child's daily routine, will usually be made by the parent who has the child that day.

9.23 If my spouse is awarded primary physical custody of my child, how much time will our child spend with me?

Parenting time schedules for noncustodial parents can vary greatly from case to case. As in the determination of custody, the best interest of the child is what a court considers in determining the parenting time schedule.

Among the factors that can impact a parenting time schedule are the history of parenting time, the age and needs of the child, and the parents' work schedules.

If you and your spouse are willing to reach your own agreement about the parenting time schedule, you are likely to be more satisfied with it than with one imposed by a judge. Because the two of you know your child's needs, your family traditions, and your personal preferences, you can design a plan uniquely suited to your child's best interests—if you can reach agreement.

If you and your spouse are unable to reach an agreement on a parenting time schedule, either on your own or with the assistance of your lawyers or a mediator, the judge will decide the schedule.

9.24 What is a parenting plan?

A parenting plan is a document detailing how you and your spouse will be parenting your child after the divorce. It is usually entered in the court record as an order. Among the issues addressed in a parenting plan are:

- Custody, both legal and physical
- Parenting time, including specific times for:
    - Regular school year
    - Holidays
    - Birthdays
    - Mother's Day and Father's Day
    - Summer
    - School breaks
- Phone access to the child
- Communication regarding the child
- Access to records regarding the child
- Notice regarding parenting time
- Attendance at the child's activities
- Decision making regarding the child
- Exchange of information such as addresses, phone numbers, and care providers

Detailed parenting plans are usually good for children and parents. They increase clarity for the parents, provide security for the child in knowing what to expect, reduce conflict, and lower the risk of needing to return to court for a modification of your divorce decree.

9.25 I don't think it's safe for my children to have any contact with my spouse. How can I prove this to the judge?

Keeping your children safe is so important that this discussion with your attorney requires immediate attention. Talk with your attorney about a plan for the protection of you and your children. Options might include a protection order, supervised visitation, or certain restrictions on your spouse's parenting time.

Give your attorney a complete history of the facts upon which you base your belief that your children are not safe with the other parent. While the most recent facts are often the most relevant, it is important that your attorney have a clear picture of the background as well.

Your attorney also needs information about your spouse, such as whether your spouse is or has been:

- Using alcohol or drugs
- Treated for alcohol or drug use
- Arrested, charged, or convicted of crimes of violence
- In possession of firearms
- Subject to a protection order for harassment or violence

Your attorney may inform you that you do not have enough evidence to support a claim that your spouse is a threat to the safety of you or the children. Do not take this as your attorney not caring. He or she has experience in knowing what the court will consider relevant and what it will not.

However, make sure you have an attorney who understands your concerns for the welfare of your children. If your attorney is not taking your worry about the safety of your children seriously, you may be better served by a lawyer with a greater understanding of the issues in your case. Or, perhaps your perspective of the problem is inaccurate. As with medical matters, if you are not sure about the advice you have been given, it is often appropriate to seek out a second opinion.

9.26 My spouse keeps saying he'll get custody because there were no witnesses to his abuse and I can't prove it. Is he right?

Probably not. Most domestic violence is not witnessed by others and judges know this. If you have been a victim of abusive behavior by your spouse, or if you have witnessed your children as victims, your testimony is likely to be the most compelling evidence.

Be sure to tell your attorney about anyone who may have either seen your spouse's behavior or spoken to you or your children right after an abusive incident. They may be important witnesses in your custody case. Also inform your lawyer of any other evidence that might exist.

9.27 I am concerned about protecting my child from abuse by my spouse. Which types of past abuse by my spouse are important to tell my attorney?

All of them. Keeping your child safe is your top priority. So that your attorney can help you protect your child, give him or her a full history of the following:

- Hitting, kicking, pushing, shoving, or slapping you or your child
- Sexual abuse
- Threats to harm you or the child
- Threats to abduct your child, or actually doing so
- Destruction of property
- Torture or abuse of pets
- Requiring your child to keep secrets

The process of writing down past events may help you to remember other incidents of abuse that you had forgotten. Be as complete as possible.

9.28 What documents or items should I give my attorney to help prove the history of domestic violence by my spouse?

The following may be useful exhibits if your case goes to court:

- Photographs of injuries
- Photographs of damaged property
- Abusive or threatening notes, letters, or e-mails
- Abusive or threatening voice messages
- Your journal entries about abuse
- Police reports
- Medical records
- Court records
- Criminal and traffic records
- Damaged property, such as torn clothing

Tell your attorney which of these you have or are able to obtain. Ask your lawyer whether others can be acquired through a subpoena or other means.

9.29 How can I get the other parent's visitation to be supervised?

If you are concerned about the safety of your children when they are with the other parent, talk to your lawyer. It may be that a protection order is warranted to terminate or limit contact with your children. Alternatively, it is possible to ask the judge to consider certain court orders intended to better protect your children.

Ask your attorney whether, under the facts of your case, the judge would consider any of the following court orders:

- Supervised visits
- Exchanges of the children in a public place
- Parenting class for the other parent
- Anger management or other rehabilitative program for the other parent
- A prohibition against drinking by the other parent when with the children

Judges have differing approaches to cases where children are at risk. Recognize that there are also often practical considerations, such as cost or the availability of people to supervise visits.

Urge your attorney to advocate zealously for court orders to protect your children from harm by the other parent.

9.30 I want to talk to my spouse about our child, but all she wants to do is argue. How can I communicate without it always turning into a fight?

If conflict is high between you and your spouse, consider the following:

- Ask your lawyer to help you obtain a court order for custody and parenting time that is specific and detailed. This lowers the amount of necessary communication between you and your spouse.
- Put as much information in writing as possible.
- Consider using e-mail, mail, or fax, especially for less urgent communication with your spouse.
- Avoid criticisms of your spouse's parenting.
- Avoid telling your spouse how to parent.
- Be factual, and business like.
- Acknowledge to your spouse the good parental qualities he or she displays, such as being concerned, attentive, or generous.
- Keep your child out of any conflicts.

By focusing on your own behavior, conflict with your spouse has the potential to decrease.

9.31 What if the child is not returned from parenting time at the agreed-upon time? Should I call the police?

Calling the police should be done only as a last resort if you feel that your child is at risk for abuse, neglect, or abduction or if you have been advised by your attorney that such a call is warranted. The involvement of law enforcement officials in parental conflict can result in far greater trauma to a child than a late return at the end of a parenting time.

The appropriate response to a child not being returned according to a court order depends upon the circumstances. If the problem is a recurring one, talk to your attorney regarding your options. It may be that a change in the schedule would be in the best interest of your child.

Regardless of the behavior of the other parent, make every effort to keep your child out of any conflicts between the adults.

9.32 If I have primary physical custody, may I move out of state without the permission of the court?

No. A custodial parent must obtain either the other parent's written consent or permission of the court prior to moving out of state with a child. If your former spouse agrees to your move, contact your attorney for preparing and submitting the necessary documents to your former spouse.

If your former spouse objects to your move, you must apply to the court for permission, give your spouse notice of the application, and have a court hearing for the judge to decide.

To obtain the court's permission, you must first prove that you have a legitimate reason for the move, such as a better job or a transfer of your new spouse's employment. You must also prove that the move is in the best interest of your child. Temporary removal of a child in such cases is ordinarily not granted. It may be important to expedite your case so you will have a final court ruling determining whether you may move out of state with your child before your planned move date.

For a detailed review of the standards and cases governing relocation ("move") cases, see the resources posted at http://willicklawgroup.com/child-custody-and-visitation/.

9.33 What factors does the court consider when determining the best interest of the child in a relocation case?

In determining your child's best interest, the court may consider many factors. These can include your child's ties to Nevada, the quality of the community you want to move to, and your child's relationship with the other parent.

In Nevada, the first factor the court considers is the *threshold question*, the question that must first be answered before any others can be asked. The first question deals with whether the custodial parent "has demonstrated that an actual advantage will be realized by both the children and the custodial parent in moving to a location so far removed from the current residence that weekly visitation by the noncustodial parent is virtually precluded."

If the custodial parent satisfies that threshold requirement, then the court must weigh additional factors and their impact on all members of the family, including the extent to which the compelling interests of each member of the family are accommodated:

- The extent to which the move is likely to improve the quality of life for both the children and the custodial parent
- Whether the custodial parent's motives are honorable, and not designed to frustrate or defeat visitation rights accorded to the noncustodial parent
- Whether, if permission to remove is granted, the custodial parent will comply with any substitute visitation orders issued by the court
- Whether the noncustodian's motives are honorable in resisting the motion for permission to remove, or to what extent, if any, the opposition is intended to secure a financial advantage in the form of ongoing support obligations or otherwise
- Whether, if removal is allowed, there will be a realistic opportunity for the noncustodial parent to maintain a visitation schedule that will adequately foster and preserve the parental relationship with the child

For each of these factors, there are multiple detailed questions, called *subfactors,* that must be answered.

If you're considering an out-of-state move, talk to your attorney immediately. Do so even if you have not finalized your plans. There are important facts for you to gather as soon as possible about potential housing, school, and day care, in both the present and any intended other location.

9.34 After the divorce, can my spouse legally take our children out of the state during parenting time? Out of the country?

It depends upon the terms of the court order as set forth in your decree. If you are concerned about your children being taken out of Nevada with the other parent, you may want to include some of these decree provisions regarding out-of-state travel with your child:

- Limits on the duration or distance for out-of-state travel with the child
- Notice and itinerary requirements
- Information on phone numbers
- Information on physical addresses
- E-mail address contact information
- Possession of the child's passport with the court
- Posting of bond by the other parent prior to travel
- Requiring a court order for travel outside the country

Although judges are not ordinarily concerned about short trips across state lines, you should let your attorney know if you are concerned that your child may be abducted by the other parent so that reasonable safeguards may be put in place.

9.35 If I am not given custody, what rights do I have regarding medical records and medical treatment for my child?

Regardless of which parent has physical custody, if the parents have joint legal custody they both should have access to the medical records of their children and the right to make emergency medical decisions.

9.36 If I'm not the primary caregiver, how will I know what's going on at my child's school? What rights to records do I have there?

Regardless of your custodial status (as long as you have at least joint legal custody), you have a right to have access to your child's school records.

Develop a relationship with your child's teachers and the school staff. Request to be put on the school's mailing list for all notices. Find out what is necessary for you to do to get copies of important school information and report cards. Today, much of that information is online and requires only a password.

Communicate with the other parent to both share and receive information about your child's progress in school. This will enable you to support your child and one another through any challenging periods of your child's education. It also enables you to share a mutual pride in your child's successes.

Regardless of which parent has primary custody, your child will benefit by your involvement in his or her education through your participation in parent-teacher conferences, attendance at school events, help with school homework, and positive communication with the other parent.

9.37 What if my child does not want to go for his or her parenting time? Can my former spouse force the child to go?

If your child is resisting going with the other parent, it can first be helpful to determine the underlying reason. Consider these questions:

- What is your child's stated reason for not wanting to go?
- Does your child appear afraid, anxious, or sad?
- Do you have any actual concerns regarding your child's safety while with the other parent?
- Have you prepared your child for being with the other parent, speaking about the experience with enthusiasm and encouragement?
- Is it possible your child is perceiving your anxiety about the situation and is consequently having the same reaction?
- Have you provided support for your child's transition to the other home, such as completing fun activities in your home well in advance of the other parent's starting time for parenting?
- Have you spoken to the other parent about your child's behavior?

- Can you provide anything that will make your child's time with the other parent more comfortable, such as a favorite toy or blanket?
- Have you established clear routines that support your child to be ready to go with the other parent with ease, such as packing a back pack or saying good-bye to a family pet?

The reason for a child's reluctance to go with the other parent may be as simple as being sad about leaving you or as serious as being a victim of abuse in the other parent's home. It is important to look at this situation closely to determine the best response.

Judges treat compliance with court orders for parenting time seriously. If one parent believes that the other is intentionally interfering with parenting time or the parent-child relationship, it can result in further litigation, or even a loss of custody. At the same time, you want to know that your child is safe. Talk with your attorney about the best approach in your situation.

9.38 What steps can I take to prevent my spouse from getting the children in the event of my death?

Unless the other parent is not fit to have custody, he or she will have first priority in the event of your death.

All parents should have a will naming a guardian for their children. In the event you do not intend to name the other parent, talk with your attorney. Seek counsel about how to best document and preserve the evidence that will be needed to prove that the other parent is unfit to have custody in the event of your death so that those documents, records, etc., will be available.

10

Child Support

Whether you will be paying or receiving child support, it is often the subject of much worry. Will I receive enough support to take care of my children? Will I have enough money to live on after I pay my child support? How will I make ends meet?

Most parents want to provide for their children. Today, the child-support laws make it possible for parents to have a better understanding of their obligation to support their children. The mechanisms for both payment and receipt of child support are more clearly defined, and help is available for collecting support if it's not paid.

The Nevada Child Support Guidelines are fairly straightforward and simple, making it easy to calculate child support in most cases.

10.1 What determines whether I will get child support?

Whether you will receive child support depends upon a number of factors. These may include how much time your child is living in your household, which parent has custody, and each parent's ability to pay support.

If your spouse is not the biological or adoptive parent of your child, it is possible you will not receive child support from your spouse. If your spouse has very limited income, the support ordered may be as little as $100 per month.

If you have primary physical custody of your child, it is likely your spouse will be ordered to pay support for any children born or adopted during your marriage. However, if you have joint custody of the children—defined by the Nevada Supreme Court as a split of between 40 and 60 percent of custodial time between the parents (about a four days to three days time share)—your child support will be determined by comparing the gross incomes of the parties.

10.2 Can I get temporary support while waiting for custody to be decided?

A judge has authority to enter a temporary order for custody and child support. This order ordinarily remains in place until a final decree establishing custody is entered. In most cases a hearing for temporary custody and support can be held shortly after the filing of the complaint for divorce.

10.3 What is *temporary support* and how soon can I get it?

Temporary support is paid for the support of a spouse or a child. It is paid sometime after the divorce complaint is filed and continues until your final decree of divorce is entered by the court (or your case is dismissed). Because there are a number of steps to getting a temporary child support order, don't delay in discussing your need for support with your lawyer.

If you are in need of temporary support, talk to your attorney at your first opportunity. If you and your spouse (with or without assistance of the lawyers) are unable to agree upon the amount of temporary support to be paid each month, it is likely that your attorney will file a motion for temporary support, asking the judge to decide how much the support should be and when it will start.

Normally, an order is made retroactive to whenever the motion for support was filed, but a court could decide to only have support paid from the time of the hearing going forward. Child support may be ordered for up to four years prior to the date of a motion requesting it, if the parents do not reside together and one parent provided the cost of care, support, education, and maintenance of the child.

The following are the common steps in the process:

- You discuss your need for a temporary child support with your lawyer.
- An attempt is made to negotiate payment of temporary support without the need for litigation.

- Your lawyer prepares the necessary documents (usually, a motion and a financial disclosure form).
- A temporary support hearing is held.
- The temporary order is signed by the judge.
- If your spouse is unreliable in payments to you, a wage withholding can be initiated. Your spouse's employer is notified to begin withholding support payments from your spouse's paychecks and sending the money directly to you.
- If you are utilizing a wage withholding, your spouse's employer will send the support as directed by the court order. Usually, the money will come directly to you, but it may be sent through the district attorney's office. In Nevada, the *district attorney* is the child-support collection agency.
- If your support is being passed through the district attorney, they will send the money to you. They charge a once-per-year fee of $50 for managing your account.

10.4 How soon does my spouse have to start paying support for the children?

Your spouse may begin paying you support voluntarily at any time. A temporary order for support will give you the right to collect the support if your spouse stops paying. Talk to your lawyer about court hearings for temporary support in your county. You may have to wait for a week or two (or longer) before your temporary hearing can be held. While payments are typically ordered to begin immediately or shortly after the hearing, it is possible that the judge will not order child support to start until the first of the following month.

10.5 How is the amount of child support I'll receive or pay figured?

The Nevada Child Support Guidelines are governed by statute and are adjusted once per year—on July 1—with the maximums called the *presumptive max* or *cap.* These guidelines are used whether you have primary physical custody of your children or joint physical custody with your spouse.

They are called "presumptive" because the court has the discretion to order more or less than the guideline amount depending on a number of factors that may include:

- The custodial time share of the parties
- The gross income of the parties
- Whether one party is providing health insurance for the minor children
- The cost of child care and who is paying it
- Any special educational needs of the child
- The age of the child
- The legal responsibility of the parents for the support of others
- The value of services contributed by either parent
- Any public assistance paid to support the child.
- Any expenses reasonably related to the mother's pregnancy and confinement
- The cost of transportation of the child for visitation if the custodial parent moved with the child out of state and the noncustodial parent remained in Nevada
- The amount of time that the child spends with each parent
- Other necessary expenses for the benefit of the child
- The relative incomes of the parents

According to the guidelines, both parents have a duty to contribute to the support of their children. When a judge orders an amount of support that is different from the guideline amount, it is often referred to as a *deviation*.

You can review the current child support tables at http://willicklawgroup.com/child-support/. Posted at the same place are worksheets for calculating child support for primary or joint custody cases, a spreadsheet showing child support for one to five children by hourly wages, and a lot of other background, statutory links, articles, and explanation relating to child support in Nevada.

10.6 Will the type of custody arrangement or the amount of parenting time I have impact the amount of child support I receive?

Yes. Sharing physical custody can dramatically lower—or eliminate—child-support amounts, unless the parents' incomes are very widely different. For this reason, it is essential that you discuss child support with your attorney prior to reaching any agreements with your spouse regarding custody or parenting time.

To predict the impact that a change in custody would have on child support in a given case, refer to worksheets for calculating child support for primary or joint custody cases posted at http://willicklawgroup.com/child-support/.

If you intend to mediate custody or parenting time, be sure to talk with your attorney in advance regarding how various possible custody arrangements would affect child support.

10.7 Is overtime pay considered in the calculation of child support?

Yes, if the overtime is "substantial and can be determined accurately." Those terms are not well defined, but roughly mean that the overtime income is more than a trivial sum, a regular part of employment, and actually expected to be earned on some regular basis. The judge can consider work history, the degree of control the party earning it actually has to control overtime, and the nature of the field of work.

10.8 Will rental income be factored into my child support?

Yes. Income from other sources may be considered in determining the amount of child support. The relevant statute says that courts are to look at "the total amount of income received each month from any source." Special rules apply to the self-employed, who get to deduct "legitimate business expenses" but not personal income taxes, retirement benefits contributions, or personal expenses, before figuring their income for child-support purposes.

10.9 My spouse has a college degree but refuses to get a job. Will the court consider this in determining the amount of child support?

The *earning capacity* of your spouse may be considered instead of current income. The court can look at your spouse's work history, education, skills, health, and job opportunities and can even "impute" (assign) a monthly income.

If you believe your spouse is earning substantially less than the income she or he is capable of earning (this is known as *willful underemployment*), provide your attorney with details. Ask about making a case for child support based on earning capacity instead of actual income.

10.10 Will I get the child support directly from my spouse or from the state?

This depends on the order from the court and on your spouse's willingness to actually pay the support on time. If your spouse makes payments timely, the payments are usually made directly. However, if your spouse is habitually late with payments, an order for a wage assignment or payment through the district attorney may be required.

10.11 If my spouse sends in child-support payments to the district attorney, how quickly will I get the money?

A number of factors affect how quickly your child-support payment will be paid to you after it is received by the district attorney, such as whether it is an out-of-state check or a certified check.

The district attorney amends its procedures from time to time in an effort to increase efficiency. That office has moved to putting money on a debit card that is issued to the support recipient when the wage assignment is started. It may take over thirty days for the first payment to appear on the card, but after that, it should appear within three to five business days after the due date each month. Usually, even if your spouse is having deductions from each pay period, you will see the money deposited to the card only once per month.

10.12 How soon can I expect my child-support payments to start arriving?

A number of factors may affect the date on which you will begin receiving your child support. Here are the usual steps in the process:

- A child-support amount and start date for the support are decided either by agreement between you and your spouse or by the judge.
- Either your attorney or your spouse's attorney prepares the court order.
- The attorney who did not write the court order reviews and approves it.
- The court order is taken to the judge for signature.
- If a wage withholding is ordered, your spouse's employer is served with the order so that support will be withheld from future paychecks.
- Your spouse's employer withholds the support from the paycheck.
- The child support is transferred by the employer to you directly or to the district attorney's office.
- The district attorney issues you a debit card and funds the card with the payment. All future payments will be placed on this same card.

As you can see, there are a lot of steps in this process. Plan your budget knowing that the initial payment of child support might be delayed as much as thirty to forty-five days, or sometimes longer.

10.13 Will some amount of child support be withheld from every paycheck?

It depends upon the employer's policy and how the employee is paid. If support is due on the first of the month, the employer has the full month to withhold the amount ordered to be paid. If an employer issues paychecks twice a month, it is possible that half of the support will be withheld from each check and then sent to the district attorney once per month.

If an employer issues checks every other week (twenty-six times per year), the child support will be calculated to take out the same amount each pay period. For example, if child support is $500 per month, that would be $6,000 per year or $230.77 per pay period.

10.14 If my spouse has income other than from an employer, is it still possible to get a court order to withhold my child support from his income?

Yes. Child support can be automatically withheld from most sources of income. These may include unemployment, worker's compensation, retirement plans, and investment income. The procedures to obtain the necessary orders vary somewhat.

10.15 The person I am divorcing is not the biological parent of my child. Can I still collect child support from my spouse?

Perhaps. Your spouse may be ordered to pay child support under certain circumstances. Among the factors the court will consider is whether your spouse has been acting in the role of a parent to your child.

Discuss the facts of your case in detail with your lawyer. When you are clear about what will be in the best interest of your child, your attorney can support you in developing a strategy for your case which takes into consideration not only child support but also the future relationship of your spouse with your child.

10.16 Can I collect child support from both the biological parent and the adoptive parent of my child?

When your child was adopted, the biological parent's duty to support your child ended. However, it may be possible for you to collect past-due child support from the period of time before the adoption.

10.17 What happens with child support when our children go to other parent's home for summer vacation? Is child support still due?

It depends. Whether child support is adjusted during extended parenting times with the noncustodial parent depends upon the court order in your case. However, most court orders in Nevada do not adjust for vacation time with the noncustodial parent.

10.18 After the divorce, if I choose to live with my new partner rather than marry, can I still collect child support?

Yes. Support for a child does not terminate based on your future relationships unless those relationships require a change in custody or other major change in circumstance, such as a termination of parental rights or adoption.

It is possible for your economic circumstances in a new relationship to be considered in determining the "relative income of the parties" in a child-support modification proceeding. While a parent's gross income for guideline child support does not include the income of either a new spouse or an adult cohabitant, the contributions of either to the household expenses can be considered as a basis for deviation from the statutory formula.

10.19 Can I still collect child support if I move to another state?

Yes. A move out of state will not end your right to receive child support. However, the amount of child support could be changed if other circumstances change, such as income or costs for exercising parenting time. If everyone leaves the state, future modifications could be based on the child support laws existing elsewhere. For background, see http://willicklawgroup.com/child-support/.

Talk with your lawyer to determine what factors could change the amount of child support you are receiving or paying.

10.20 Can I expect to continue to receive child support if I remarry?

Yes. Your child support will continue even if you remarry.

10.21 How long can I expect to receive child support?

Under Nevada law, child support is ordinarily ordered to be paid until the child dies, marries, is emancipated (becomes self supporting), or reaches the age of eighteen (or nineteen if still in high school). However, if the child-support order is from another state and is just being collected in Nevada, the originating state law would govern the duration of child support.

10.22 Does interest accrue on past-due child support?

Yes. Nevada requires statutory interest of the prime rate at the largest in-state bank plus 2 percent on any court-ordered judgment. Additionally, the state legislature has mandated that an additional 10 percent per annum penalty be assessed on any child-support payment that becomes and remains overdue for thirty days. See http://willicklawgroup.com/interest-penalties/.

Additionally, there is no *statute of limitations* on overdue child support that came due after 1981. If your spouse is not paying the required amounts, seek the help of a qualified attorney to assist in the proper calculation of the arrearage (past-due amount) and its collection. Be sure your lawyer is well versed in this subject. Many attorneys in Nevada—and the district attorney's office—calculate the arrearage interest and penalty incorrectly. For an explanation, see http://willicklawgroup.com/actual-calculation-differences/.

10.23 What can I do if my former spouse refuses to pay child support?

In Nevada, you have several options. You can use a private attorney to seek the aid of the court in collecting child support. The advantage of using private counsel in family court is that you generally get much faster results, calculation of interest and penalties, and you may request that your spouse pay your attorney's fees—the law presumes that fees will be awarded if past-due child support (referred to as "arrearages") is owed.

If you can't afford an attorney, you can seek the aid of a *pro bono* (for free) attorney through the local *pro bono* project. You can also seek assistance through the district attorney's office (but, as explained above, under their present procedures the calculation of interest and penalties by the district attorney will be incorrect).

The judge may order payment of both the current amount of support and an additional amount to be paid each month until the arrearages are paid in full.

You may request that your former spouse's federal tax refunds be seized and sent to you through the district attorney.

Driver's licenses (and other kinds of state-issued licenses) may also be suspended if a parent falls behind in child-support payments. However, if there is a payment plan for the payment of arrearages, then licenses will normally not be suspended.

Your former spouse may also be found in *contempt of court* if the failure to pay support is intentional. Possible consequences include being fined or jailed.

In short, if you are not receiving child support, you have three options:

- Call your attorney.
- Call the *pro bono* project in the county where you reside.
- Contact the district attorney's office for assistance.

10.24 At what point will the district attorney help me collect back child support, and what methods do they use?

It depends. When the district attorney will help you collect back child support and the methods they will use can depend upon the amount of back child support owed.

Driver's, recreational, and professional licenses can be suspended if child support is owed. If more than $500 in back support is due, state or federal income tax refunds can be intercepted. Where more than $5,000 is owed, a passport can be denied.

In some cases, failure to pay child support can result in a jail sentence for contempt, or outright criminal prosecution for nonsupport.

You must initiate contact with the district attorney's office if you want help from that agency in collecting child support.

10.25 I live outside Nevada. Will the money I spend on airline tickets to see my children impact my child support?

It might. If you expect to spend large sums of money for transportation in order to have parenting time with your children, talk to your attorney about how this might be taken into consideration when determining the amount of child support to be paid.

10.26 After the divorce, can my former spouse substitute buying sprees with the child for child-support payments?

No. Purchases of gifts and clothing for a child do not relieve your former spouse from an obligation to pay you child support.

10.27 Are expenses such as child care supposed to be taken out of my child support?

Normally no, although it depends on the court order. Child-care expenses can be considered separate from child support. However, if the court takes child-care costs into consideration at the time the original order is entered, then child care paid by either parent after that order will have no effect on the child support due.

Make sure you discuss this issue with your attorney before any temporary or final child-support orders are entered.

10.28 Can my spouse deduct money from child-support payments for money my spouse claims I owe in reimbursement for other expenses?

The short answer is "No." Your spouse is required to deal with non-child support matters and obligations separately from child support. If your spouse "deducts" amounts you supposedly owe him or her from child support that should have been paid, talk to your lawyer. It is possible that a request for the deducted money will cause it to be paid, or that a motion for child-support arrearages can be filed to recover the sums wrongfully withheld—plus interest, penalties, and attorney's fees, if appropriate.

10.29 Can my spouse be required by the decree to pay for our child's private elementary and high school education?

Probably not. Some judges hold differing views on the subject, but Nevada law makes no specific provision for private education tuition, beside the "deviation factor" that says a court may consider "any special educational needs of the child" in setting support. Where there was a history of private education before the divorce, some judges consider it appropriate to order that such education continue after the divorce. Additionally, some parents agree to include a provision in the decree for payment of such tuition because both of them believe it is important for their child.

If you want your spouse to share such expenses for your child, talk it over with your lawyer. Be sure to provide your attorney with all known or projected information regarding tuition, fees, and other expenses related to private education.

10.30 Can my spouse be required by the decree to contribute financially to our child's college education?

Unlike some states, Nevada law does not include any provision permitting a court to order payment of postsecondary education expenses (such as college) over the objection of a parent. However, if you or your spouse or both agree to pay this expense, it can be included in the final decree and it will be an enforceable court order. Such a provision is ordinarily included in a divorce decree only as a result of a negotiated settlement.

If your decree includes a provision for payment of college education expenses, be sure it is specific. Terms to consider include:

- What expenses are included? For example, tuition, room and board, books, fees, travel, etc.
- Is there a limit? For example, up to the level of the cost of attendance at the University of Nevada Las Vegas, or a certain dollar amount.
- When and to whom (the other parent, the child, or the school) is the payment due?
- For what period of time does it continue?
- Are there any limits on the type of education that will be paid for, or the number of years, or any age limits by which such an education must be completed?

The greater the clarity in such a provision, the lower the risk is for misunderstanding or conflict arising years later.

11

Alimony

The mere mention of the word *alimony* (also referred to as *spousal support*) might stir your emotions and start your stomach churning. If your spouse has filed for divorce and is seeking alimony, you might see it as a double injustice—your marriage is ending and you feel like you have to pay for it, too. If you are seeking spousal support, you might feel hurt and confused that your spouse is resistant to helping support you, even though you interrupted your career to stay home and care for your children.

Learning more about Nevada's laws on alimony can help you move from an emotional reaction to one based on the reality of possible outcomes in your case. Uncertainty about the precise amount of alimony that may be awarded or the number of years it might be paid is not unusual. Work closely with your lawyer. Be open to possibilities. Try looking at the issue from your spouse's perspective.

With the help of your lawyer, you will determine the best course of action to take toward obtaining an alimony decision you can live with after your divorce is over.

11.1 Which gets calculated first, child support or alimony?

There is no Nevada statute on the subject.

Often, when one party is paying both child support and alimony, child support is determined first, and spousal support is determined from the income that is available after the amount of child support is deducted. This is often how temporary orders are determined.

But it can also go the other way. Once a permanent order is in place, any alimony being paid by a spouse might be deducted from the spouse's income before figuring what child support is owed. Also, if a party receiving alimony has to pay child support, the alimony could be considered as part of the income on which child support is based.

11.2 What's the difference between *spousal support, alimony,* and *maintenance*?

In Nevada, *alimony* and *spousal support* have the same meaning. Sometimes, the word *maintenance* is used as well.

It is typical to refer to payments from one spouse to the other before a divorce is entered as *temporary spousal support.* Usually, the word "alimony" is used to describe payments made after the divorce is final.

But lawyers and courts are not required to use specific terms, and they sometimes also refer to alimony to be paid after divorce for only a specific length of time as temporary spousal support. They might also use the word "maintenance" to describe payments made before or after divorce.

11.3 Are there different types of alimony?

Yes. In Nevada, a court can award alimony for a fixed or indefinite period of time to assist a party with maintaining a certain lifestyle or to get on with life after divorce. This can be called *general alimony, reimbursement alimony, compensatory alimony, temporary alimony, permanent alimony,* or just *alimony.*

Such an award might also be labeled as *modifiable* or *unmodifiable,* indicating whether it is intended that the award can be changed (made greater or smaller, or for a shorter or longer time) after the divorce decree is entered.

A spouse can also be awarded alimony to assist with obtaining new skills to be self supporting after the divorce. This is known as *rehabilitative alimony,* and is almost always made payable in a specific amount for a specified amount of time.

The court also has the power to "set aside" the separate property of one spouse for the support of the other. This is known as *lump sum alimony* or (sometimes) *alimony in gross.*

A lot more information about the kinds of alimony that might be awarded in Nevada, the case law explaining it, and the rules concerning when it might be awarded, denied, or altered, is discussed in the explanation and articles posted on our website at http://willicklawgroup.com/spousal-supportalimony/.

11.4 How will I know if I am eligible to receive alimony?

Talk with your attorney about whether you are a candidate for alimony.

The opinions of Nevada judges about awarding alimony vary greatly. Among the factors that may affect your eligibility to receive alimony are:

- The length of your marriage
- Your contributions to the marriage, including interruption of your career for the care of children or to support your spouse's career
- Your education, work history, health, age, income, and earning capacity
- Your overall financial situation compared to that of your spouse
- Your need for support
- Your spouse's ability to pay support

Every case concerning alimony is unique. Providing your lawyer with clear and detailed information about the facts of your marriage and current situation will increase the likelihood of a fair outcome for you.

However, one thing that you must keep in mind is that alimony is never guaranteed. If no alimony is awarded at the time of your divorce, you can't come back later to get it. In Nevada law, there is only one bite at this apple.

11.5 What information should I provide to my attorney if I want alimony?

If your attorney advises you that you may be a candidate for alimony, be sure to provide complete facts about your situation, including:

- A history of any interruptions in your education or career for the benefit of your spouse, including transfers or moves due to your spouse's employment
- A history of the interruptions in your education or career for raising children, including periods during which you worked part time
- Your complete educational background, including the dates of your schooling or training and degrees earned
- Your work history, including the names of your employers, the dates of your employment, your duties, your pay, and the reasons you left
- Any direct or indirect contribution you made to the career of your spouse that is expected to continue generating income in the future
- Any pensions or other benefits lost due to the interruption of your career for the benefit of the marriage.
- Your health history, including any current diagnoses, treatments, limitations, and medications
- Your monthly living expenses, including anticipated future expenses such as health insurance and tax on alimony
- A complete list of the debts for you and your spouse
- Income for you and your spouse, including all sources

Also include any other facts that might support your need for alimony, such as other contributions you made to the marriage, upcoming medical treatment, or a lack of jobs in the field in which you were formerly employed.

No two alimony cases are alike. The better the information your lawyer has about your situation, the easier it will be for him or her to assess your case for alimony.

11.6 My spouse told me that because I had an affair during the marriage, I have no chance to get alimony even though I quit my job and have cared for our children for many years. Is it true that I have no case?

That is not the law in Nevada. Your right to alimony will be based upon many factors, but having an affair is not a bar to getting spousal support. The Nevada Supreme Court has stated that such "fault" factors may not be considered by a court in deciding alimony. Nevada is a no-fault state, so no matter the reason for a divorce, alimony is to be determined on economic, not moral, grounds.

11.7 How is the amount of alimony calculated?

Unlike child support, there is no specific formula for determining the amount of alimony. A judge will look at the expenses and incomes of you and your spouse, after giving consideration to the payment and receipt of child support.

Under current law, judges are required to consider a number of factors in determining whether and how much alimony is to be awarded. Those factors are:

- The financial condition of each spouse
- The nature and value of the respective property of each spouse
- The contribution of each spouse to any property held by the spouses pursuant to section 123.030 of the *Nevada Revised Statutes*
- The duration of the marriage
- The income, earning capacity, age, and health of each spouse
- The standard of living during the marriage
- The career before the marriage of the spouse who would receive the alimony
- The existence of specialized education or training or the level of marketable skills attained by each spouse during the marriage
- The contribution of either spouse as homemaker
- The award of property granted by the court in the divorce, other than child support and alimony, to the spouse who would receive the alimony
- The physical and mental condition of each party as it relates to the financial condition, health, and ability to work of that spouse

It hardly need be said that the above statutory list is not particularly helpful in actually determining how much, if any, alimony should be awarded and, if it is awarded, for how long. Judges are given a lot of discretion to make their own decision on alimony without the benefit of specific guidelines. Consequently, an alimony ruling by a judge can be one of the most unpredictable aspects of your divorce. This is the last great "crapshoot" in Nevada family law.

A lot more information about alimony in Nevada is discussed in the explanation and articles posted on our website at http://willicklawgroup.com/spousal-supportalimony/.

11.8 My spouse makes a lot more money than he reports on our tax return, but he hides it. How can I prove my spouse's real income to show he can afford to pay alimony?

Alert your attorney to your concerns. Your lawyer can then take a number of actions to determine your spouse's actual income with greater accuracy. They are likely to include:

- More-thorough discovery
- An examination of check registers, credit card records, and bank deposits
- Review of purchases made in cash
- Inquiries about travel
- Depositions of third parties who have knowledge of income or spending by your spouse
- Subpoena of records of places where your spouse has made large purchases or received income
- Comparison of income claimed with expenses paid

Lawyers sometimes hire forensic accountants or other professionals to assist in uncovering true income in such cases.

Working with your lawyer, you may be able to build a case to establish your spouse's actual income as greater than what is shown on your tax returns. If you filed joint tax returns, discuss with your lawyer any other implications to you of erroneous information on those returns.

11.9 I want to be sure the records on the alimony I pay are accurate, especially for tax purposes. What's the best way to ensure this?

Always pay by a method that is traceable. Write a check, get a money order, or wire funds with a printed receipt.

Copies of canceled checks and paid money orders are acceptable to both the IRS and to the court as proof that you paid your alimony. You certainly do not want your spouse coming back after five years and claiming that you haven't paid. These receipts will protect you.

Keep these receipts forever! Or, at least until there is no possibility that any court or agency might wish to review evidence of payment. If uncertain, ask your lawyer.

11.10 How is the purpose of alimony different from the payment of my property settlement?

Spousal support and the division of property serve two distinct purposes, even though many of the factors for determining them are the same. The purpose of alimony is to pay for a party's continued support after divorce, whereas the purpose of a property division is to distribute the marital assets between you and your spouse as required by law. See chapter 12 for information regarding the division of property.

11.11 How long can I expect to receive alimony?

Like your right to receive alimony at all, how long you will receive alimony will depend upon the facts of your case and the judge's philosophy toward alimony. Awards of lifetime alimony in Nevada are relatively rare. You may receive only temporary alimony, or you may receive alimony for several years. In general, the longer your marriage, and the greater the gap between the post-divorce earnings of the parties, the stronger your case is for a long-term alimony award.

Talk to your attorney about the facts of your case to get a clearer picture of the possible outcomes in your situation. Unless you and your spouse agree otherwise, or the court specifically orders, your alimony will terminate upon your remarriage or the death of either of you.

11.12 Does remarriage affect my alimony?

Normally, yes. Under Nevada law, your alimony ends upon the remarriage or death of the person receiving alimony, but not upon the remarriage of the party paying alimony, unless the court order specifically states otherwise.

11.13 Can I continue to collect alimony if I move to a different state?

Yes. The duty of your former spouse to follow a court order to pay alimony does not end simply because either you or your former spouse move to another state, unless that condition was specifically stated in your decree.

11.14 What can I do if my spouse stops paying alimony?

If your spouse stops paying alimony, see your attorney about your options for enforcing your court order. The judge may order the support taken from a source of your spouse's income or from a financial account belonging to your spouse.

If your spouse is intentionally refusing to pay spousal support, talk to your attorney about whether pursuing a contempt of court action would be effective. In a contempt action, your spouse may be ordered to appear in court and provide evidence explaining why support has not been paid. Possible consequences for contempt of court include a jail sentence or a fine.

11.15 Can I return to court to modify alimony?

It depends. If there has been a material change in the circumstances of either you or your spouse, you may usually seek to have alimony modified. Examples include a serious illness or the loss or obtaining of a job.

A request seeking additional alimony may not be filed if the time for payment of alimony allowed under your original decree has already passed and their required payments were made.

If your divorce decree provides that your alimony order is non-modifiable, then you will not likely be able to have it modified. Also, if no award of alimony was made in the decree, you will not be entitled to receive alimony in the future.

If you think you have a basis to modify an alimony award, contact your attorney at once to be sure a timely modification request is filed with the court.

11.16 What if my ex-spouse dies before all alimony owed to me is paid?

First, it depends on what the court order provides. While Nevada law is not completely clear, if the order calls for payments to continue after, or to be paid regardless of, the death of the person paying alimony (for example, for a certain amount to be paid no matter who lives for how long) it is possible that a claim may be made against the estate of the deceased person for the amount remaining to be paid.

12

Division of Property

You never imagined that you would face losing the house you and your spouse so happily moved into—the house where you celebrated family traditions and that you spent countless hours making "home." Your spouse wants it and your lawyer says it might have to be sold.

During a divorce, you will decide whether you or your spouse will take ownership of everything from bathroom towels to the stock portfolio. Suddenly you find yourself having a strong attachment to that lamp in the family room or the painting in the hallway. Why does the coin collection suddenly take on new meaning?

Do your best to reach agreement regarding dividing household goods. Enlist the support of your attorney in deciding which assets should be valued by an expert, such as the family business or real estate. From tax consequences to replacement value, there are many factors to consider in deciding whether to fight to keep an asset, to give it to your spouse, to split it, or to have it sold.

Like all aspects of your divorce, take one step at a time. By starting with the items most easily divided, you and your spouse can avoid paying lawyers to litigate the value of that 1970s album collection.

12.1 What system does Nevada use for dividing property?

Nevada is a community property state and the law provides for a presumptively equal division of the property and debts acquired during your marriage. The court may make an *unequal* distribution of property if it finds "compelling reasons" to do so. Background materials and explanations of how such a determination might be made are posted at http://willicklawgroup.com/property-rights-and-division/.

Regardless of how title is held, the court can use its discretion to make a division of the marital assets. The court will usually try to divide the property equally between the parties unless there is an agreement or "stipulation" that an unequal division is appropriate.

The court can also use its discretion to "off set" other property or waste by one party with an unequal division of community property.

12.2 What does *community property* mean, and when does the "community" begin and end?

Community property is a term used in nine states, including Nevada, under which each spouse holds a one-half interest in most property acquired during the marriage. It is a system that was brought to this country by the Spanish explorers who populated the early western states, and has remained in place since the early days of the country.

Under Nevada law, virtually all property acquired during the marriage by either spouse belongs to both spouses, regardless of who earned it or whose name it is in. Exceptions include gifts, inherited property, or an award for personal injury damages. Much more detail about what community property is and how it is divided in Nevada divorces is posted at http://willicklawgroup.com/property-rights-and-division/.

In Nevada, the "community" normally begins upon marriage, and continues until divorce. In some circumstances, a court can consider the starting date for the "community" when property began to accrue to be prior to the date of marriage, if the parties cohabited and formed a single economic unit. This area of the law is changing, so if there was any premarital cohabitation, bring it to the attention of your lawyer and provide all of the background facts as to who was living where, and what happened economically between the parties before marriage.

Unlike other states that end the community upon separation or filing for divorce, the community in Nevada normally ends at the close of the divorce trial. That means that any property and (usually) any debt incurred by either party during the divorce proceedings, which may continue for months or years, constitutes community property or debt unless a specific court order is obtained saying otherwise.

The laws affecting community property differ among the nine states in which it is effective. Make sure you speak to your attorney about how community property is dealt with in Nevada.

12.3 How is it determined who gets the house?

The first issue regarding the family home is often a determination of who will retain possession of it while the divorce is pending. Later, it must be decided whether the house will be sold or whether it will be awarded to you or your spouse.

If you and your spouse are unable to reach agreement regarding the house, the judge will decide who keeps it or whether it will be sold and the proceeds distributed between the parties.

If either party keeps the house, the equity in that property will be used as an offset to other community property to be divided. If you want to keep the house you need to decide if you can afford to maintain the property, and are willing to give your spouse cash or other property worth half the equity in the home.

12.4 Should I sell the house during the divorce proceedings?

Selling your home is a big decision. To help you decide what is right for you, ask yourself these questions:

- What will be the impact on my children if the home is sold?
- Can I afford to stay in the house and keep up its payments and expenses after the divorce?
- After the divorce, will I be willing to give the house and yard the time, money, and physical energy required for its maintenance?

- Is it necessary for me to sell the house to pay a share of the equity to my spouse, or are there other options, such as a refinance?
- Would my life be easier if I were in a smaller or simpler home?
- Would I prefer to move closer to the support of friends and family?
- What is the state of the housing market in my community?
- What are the benefits of remaining in this house?
- Can I retain the existing mortgage or will I have to refinance?
- Will I have a higher or lower interest rate (and payments) if I sell the house?
- Can I see myself living in a different home?
- Will I have the means to acquire another home?
- If I don't retain the home and my spouse asks for it, what effect will this have on my custody case?
- Will my spouse agree to the sale of the house?
- What will be the real estate commission and other expenses of sale?
- What will be the costs of preparing the house for sale?
- Can I afford to give up other community property in exchange for the equity in the home?

Selling a home is more than just a legal or financial decision. When deciding whether to sell your home, consider what is important to you in creating your life after divorce. In any event, moving forward with a sale during a divorce usually will require agreement of your spouse, or an order of the court.

12.5 What is meant by *equity* in my home?

Regardless of who is awarded your house, the court will need to balance the equity in the house between the parties. *Equity* means the difference between the value of the home and the amount owed in mortgages against the property.

For example, if the first mortgage is $50,000 and the second mortgage from a home equity loan is $10,000, the total debt owed against the house is $60,000. If your home is valued at $100,000, the equity in your home is $40,000 ($100,000 value -$60,000 in mortgages = $40,000 equity.)

If one of the parties remains in the home, the issue of how to give the other party his or her share of the equity must be considered.

12.6 How will the equity in our house be divided?

There are two questions here—whether the equity will be equally divided, and how, exactly, the money is obtained and distributed.

If all the money that went into the house—the down payment and the monthly payments—was money earned during marriage, the equity will probably be equally divided.

If one of you owned the house before marriage but made payments with community property during the marriage, the equity may be partly community and partly separate property. There are formulas to determine how to divide the equity in a home in such circumstances. Materials explaining some of how that works in divorce cases is posted at http://willicklawgroup.com/property-rights-and-division/. You should discuss any such facts with your lawyer and make sure the lawyer is fully aware of where the money to purchase the house came from.

As to the "mechanics" of distributing the equity, if your home is going to be sold, the equity in the home will most likely be divided at the time of the sale, after the costs of the sale have been paid.

If either you or your spouse will be awarded the house, there are a number of options for the other party being compensated for his or her share of the equity in the marital home. These could include:

- The spouse who does not receive the house receives other community assets to compensate for the value of the equity.
- The person who remains in the home agrees to refinance the home, immediately or at some future date, and to pay the other party his or her share of the equity.

- The parties agree that the property be sold at a future date, or upon the happening of a certain event such as the youngest child completing high school or the remarriage of the party keeping the home.

As the residence is often among the most valuable assets considered in a divorce, it is important that you and your attorney discuss the details of its disposition. These include:

- Valuation of the property
- Refinancing to remove a party from liability for the mortgage
- The dates on which certain actions should be taken, such as listing the home for sale
- The real estate agent
- Costs for preparing the home for sale
- Making mortgage payments

If you and your spouse do not agree regarding which of you will remain in the home and the related terms for division of the equity, the court will decide who keeps it or may order the property sold.

12.7 Who keeps all the household goods until the decree is signed, and after divorce?

The court will ordinarily not make any decisions about who keeps the household goods on a temporary basis, unless the parties force the court to consider the question. Most couples attempt to resolve these issues on their own rather than incur legal fees to dispute them. Remember, it can cost a lot more than those pots and pans are worth to have attorneys battle out who gets to keep them.

If the parties can't decide who is to get what household items, there are multiple ways to deal with the issue. They may utilize the "A/B" list method for distribution. One of the parties makes two lists labeled "A" and "B." Every household item is listed on one of these two lists. The party responsible for making this list should be as careful as possible to try to make the lists as equal in value as possible. Once the two lists are created, the other party gets to pick which list he or she wants, leaving the items on the other list to the party who created the list. Sometimes this is called the "you cut, I pick" method.

Alternatively, where there are multiple items of similar values, the parties can alternate picking them until they are distributed; sometimes, collections (art, coins, stamps, etc.) are divided this way when parties cannot decide who should keep them.

In some cases, an appraiser is hired to put a value on all such items, and the parties (or the court) divides them by value. This is perhaps the most expensive way of dealing with household goods and is rarely warranted.

12.8 How are assets such as cars, boats, and furniture divided, and when does this happen?

In most cases, spouses are able to reach their own agreements about how to divide personal property, such as household furnishings and vehicles.

If you and your spouse disagree about how to divide certain items, it can be wise to consider which are truly valuable to you, financially or otherwise. Perhaps some of the items can be easily replaced. Always consider whether it is a good use of your attorney's fees to argue over items of personal property.

All higher-value items—such as cars and boats—are valued and placed on a spreadsheet so that the "value" is equalized between the parties. Remember, Nevada is an equal-distribution state and if one party receives an abundance of the "things" from the marriage, the other spouse will usually get an offset in other assets such as cash.

If a negotiated settlement cannot be reached, the issue of the division of your property will be made by the judge at trial.

12.9 What is meant by a *property inventory* and how detailed should mine be?

A *property inventory* is a listing of the property you own. It may also include a brief description of the property. Nevada procedural rules require that this inventory be very detailed to ensure an equal distribution.

Discuss with your attorney how to proceed in this task. You should note that it will be important to get this inventory done early on in your divorce action, so don't delay speaking to your attorney about what you should be doing to prepare for the initial disclosures on property.

Factors to consider when creating your inventory may include:

- The extent to which you anticipate you and your spouse will disagree regarding the division of your property
- Whether you anticipate a dispute regarding the value of the property either you or your spouse is retaining
- Whether you will have continued access to the property if a later inventory is needed or whether you spouse will retain control of the property
- Whether you or your spouse are likely to disagree about which items are premarital, inherited, or gifts from someone other than your spouse

In addition to creating an inventory, your attorney may request that you prepare a list of the property that you and your spouse have already divided or a list of the items you want but your spouse has not agreed to give to you.

If you do not have continued access to your property, talk to your attorney about taking photographs or obtaining access to the property to complete your inventory.

12.10 How and when are liquid assets like bank accounts and stocks divided?

Talk with your attorney early in your case about the joint preliminary injunction (JPI) to reduce the risk that your spouse will transfer money out of financial accounts or transfer other assets, or that you will be accused of wrongfully doing so.

In many cases couples will agree to divide bank accounts equally at the outset of the case. However, this may not be advisable in your case. Discuss with your attorney whether you should keep an accounting of how you spend money used from a bank account while your divorce is in progress.

Stocks are ordinarily a part of the final agreement for the division of property and debts. If you and your spouse cannot agree on how your investments should be divided, the judge will make the decision at trial.

12.11 How is pet custody determined?

"Pet custody" is determined on a case-by-case basis. Nevada law is not well established on the matter of pet custody, and most judges appear to be of the opinion that pets are items of property to be divided between the parties like all other assets, rather than being treated like children as to whom the parties may both have rights and obligations after divorce. There is some indication, however, this the attitude, both in society generally and in the courts, may be changing. Factors that courts have considered include:

- Who held title to the pet?
- Who provided care for the pet?
- Who will best be able to meet the pet's needs?
- Has either party ever abused the pet or shown a propensity for such abuse?

Some courts have awarded the pet to one party and given the other party certain rights, such as:

- Specific periods of time to spend with the pet
- The right to care for the pet when the other person is not able to
- The right to be informed of the pet's health condition

If it is important to you to be awarded one of your family pets, discuss the matter with your attorney, and find out the current state of the law on the subject. It may be possible to reach a pet care agreement with your spouse that will allow you to share possession of and responsibility for your pets, or otherwise be satisfied with their disposition upon divorce.

However, in Nevada, at least for now, pets are property and you should presume that they are to be distributed the same way as all other property, with their value offset against other assets.

12.12 How will our property in another state be divided?

Once the Nevada court has jurisdiction over you and your spouse, it can issue orders concerning the ownership or sale of all property owned by the community no matter where it is located.

For the purposes of dividing your assets, out-of-state property is generally treated the same as property in Nevada, although it is possible that certain technical aspects of community property law could cause property that you acquired while living in another state to be treated differently under the *Braddock* or "pure borrowed law" approach. Some background information is posted at http://willicklawgroup.com/property-rights-and-division/. If there is any such property, make sure you explain to your lawyer when, where, and how that property was acquired.

Although a Nevada court cannot actually change title to property located in another state, a judge can order your spouse to sign a deed or other document to transfer title to you; procedures in the other state may be required to actually accomplish the division, sale, or transfer of that property.

12.13 I worked very hard for years to support my family while my spouse completed an advanced degree. Do I have a right to any of my spouse's future earnings?

Your contributions during the marriage are a factor to be considered in both the division of the property and debts, and any award of alimony. Be sure to give your attorney a complete history of your contributions to the marriage and ask about their impact on the outcome of your case.

12.14 Are all of the assets—such as property, bank accounts, and inheritances—that I had prior to my marriage still going to be mine after the divorce?

For the most part, yes. The presumption in Nevada is that any property that was owned strictly by one party before or during the marriage remains their sole and separate property upon divorce. In most cases the court will allow a party to retain an asset brought into the marriage, but there are questions the court will consider in making its determination such as:

- Can the premarital asset be clearly traced? For example, if you continue to own a vehicle that you brought into the marriage, it is likely that it will be awarded to you. However, if you brought a vehicle into the marriage, sold it during the marriage, and spent the proceeds on other property that was used by the community, it is less likely that the court will consider awarding you its value.

- Did you keep the property separate and titled in your name, or did you commingle it with marital assets? Premarital assets you kept separate are more likely to be awarded to you.
- Did the other spouse (or community property income) contribute to an increase in the value of the premarital asset, and can the value of that increase be proven? For example, suppose a woman owned a home prior to her marriage. After the marriage, the parties live in the home, continuing to make mortgage payments and improvements to the home. At the time of the divorce, the husband seeks a portion of the equity in the home. Nevada case law contains directions to a trial court for how to consider the value of the home at the time of the marriage, any contributions to the increase in equity made during the marriage, and the evidence of the value of those contributions.

12.15 Will I get to keep my engagement ring?

The short answer is yes. Nevada considers your engagement ring to be a conditional gift. In other words, if you were given the ring in anticipation of getting married, and you got married, you have fulfilled the condition and it became your ring as your sole and separate property.

12.16 Can I keep gifts and inheritances I received during the marriage?

Gifts and inheritances received during the marriage and premarital assets are considered separate property. Normally, all separate property owned by a party remains the property of that person after divorce. Any gifts from one spouse to the other (or from some other person) is the sole and separate property of the person receiving it. Separate property does not "count" when dividing community property. It belongs to the person who owns it and does not appear on the "marital balance sheet" of property to be divided.

Any inheritance that you receive—as long as you keep it in an account titled in your name alone—will also be treated as your sole and separate property. If the funds were "commingled"—that is, combined with community property funds–the burden may be on you to *trace* the separate property funds (that is, show how they came from a separate property source) to the satisfaction of the court in order to retain them as your separate property. The rules for tracing are technical.

There are a number of considerations when using sole and separate funds, such as an inheritance, for community purposes that may affect its treatment at divorce. Make sure you discuss this in detail with your attorney to protect and understand your rights.

12.17 If my spouse and I can't decide who gets what, who decides? Can that person's decision be contested?

If you and your spouse cannot agree on the division of your property, the judge will make the determination after considering the evidence at your trial. If either party is dissatisfied with the decision reached by the judge, an appeal to a higher court is possible.

12.18 What is a *property settlement agreement*?

A *property settlement agreement* is a written document that includes all of the financial agreements you and your spouse have reached in your divorce. This may include the division of property, debts, child support, alimony, insurance, and attorney's fees. The agreement may include every issue, or the parties may only resolve some of the issues in the case, and leave others to be determined by the judge.

The property settlement agreement may be a separate document, or it may be incorporated into the decree of divorce, which is the final court order dissolving your marriage.

A lot more information about property settlement agreements (along with other kinds of marital agreements) is discussed in the explanation and articles posted on our website at http://willicklawgroup.com/premaritalpostnuptialseparation-marital-settlement-agreements.

12.19 How are the values of property determined?

The value of some assets, like bank accounts, is usually not disputed. The value of other assets, such as homes, businesses, or personal property, is more likely to be contested.

If your case proceeds to trial, you may give your opinion of the value of property you own. You or your spouse may also have certain property appraised by an expert. In such cases it may be necessary to have the appraiser appear at trial to give testimony regarding the appraisal and the value of the asset.

If you own substantial assets for which the value is likely to be disputed, talk to your attorney early in your case about the benefits and costs of expert witnesses or other means of establishing values for proof at trial.

12.20 What does *date of valuation* mean?

Because the value of assets can go up or down while a divorce is pending, it can be necessary to determine a set date for valuing the marital assets. This is referred to as the *date of valuation.* You and your spouse may agree on the date the assets should be valued. If you cannot agree, the judge will decide the date of valuation. Though it is not always convenient, Nevada law provides that the valuation date is the closest possible date to that of the divorce.

12.21 What happens after my spouse and I approve the property settlement agreement? Do we still have to go to court?

After you and your spouse sign to approve the property settlement agreement or decree, it must still be approved by the judge, but if all issues have been resolved, you can usually "direct submit" your decree for entry by the court without the need to show up for a hearing.

Many divorces in Nevada happen without the parties ever seeing the inside of the courtroom. It is obvious that if you and your spouse can work out all of these details without going to court, the cost of the divorce will be much lower.

However, be wary of a do-it-yourself divorce which appears cheap. Many of these divorces omit issues or make mistakes of characterization, valuation, or distribution that result in lawyers spending large amounts of time and money after the divorce trying to "fix" problems that could have been avoided if the matters had been handled correctly from the beginning. As with most things, it is usually far less expensive to do something right the first time than to try to fix it after the fact.

Also avoid—like the plague—using a "paralegal service" or "quickie divorce service" to get your divorce. These services, which advertise very cheap rates, have been known to create huge problems—some of which prove to be unfixable. Sometimes, people have lost vast sums of money, or custody of children, without legitimate legal cause. Some of those cases take years to correct. Sometimes the people affected are never able to recover what was lost. The services in question have been so bad that the Nevada legislature is taking action to curb their practice in this state.

12.22 If my spouse and I think our property settlement agreement is fair, why does the judge have to approve it?

To make sure that your agreement is enforceable, the agreement must be entered by the court. The judge has a duty to ensure that an order relating to child custody appears to serve the best interest of the child. The judge is required to ensure that child support satisfies the statutes governing it, or to make findings showing why an exception is warranted. The court is required to divide community property equally, or set out written findings of a compelling reason to divide it in any other way.

A failure to do any of these things could cause the court order to be set aside, provide a basis for appeal, or result in much unnecessary post-divorce litigation.

12.23. What happens to our individual checking and savings accounts during and after the divorce?

Regardless of whose name is on the account, bank accounts are generally considered community property if the funds in those accounts were acquired during marriage.

Discuss with your attorney the benefits of the joint preliminary injunction (JPI) to protect bank accounts, how to use these accounts while the case is pending, and the date on which financial accounts should be valued, distributed, converted, or closed.

12.24 Who gets the interest from certificates of deposit, dividends from stock holdings, etc., during the divorce proceedings?

Generally, in Nevada, interest on an account follows the "character" of the account, as the "rents, profits, and issue" of the underlying property. In other words, if the account was a separate property account, the interest is separate property; if it was a community property account, the interest is community property.

Whether you or your spouse receives interest from such assets is decided as a part of the overall division of your property and debts.

12.25 Does each one of our financial accounts have to be divided in half if we agree to an equal division of our assets?

No. Rather than incurring the administrative challenges and expense of dividing each asset in half, you and your spouse can decide that one of you will take certain assets equal to the value of assets taken by the other spouse. This is the "marital balance sheet" approach. If necessary, one of you can agree to make a cash payment to the other as an equalization payment.

12.26 What factors determine whether I can get at least half of my spouse's business?

Many factors determine whether you will get a share of your spouse's business and in what form you might receive it. Among the factors the court will look at are:

- Whether your spouse owned the business prior to your marriage
- Whether there was any increase in value of the business during the marriage
- Your role, if any, in operating the business or in increasing its value

- Whether the company "retained earnings" or the owner spouse was fully and fairly compensated with income during the marriage
- The overall division of the property and debts of the community

If it is determined that the business is entirely or partially community property under Nevada law, then both spouses should normally receive half of the value of that community property interest, either as a share of the asset itself, or as a cash payment for half its value.

If you or your spouse owns a business, it is important that you work with your attorney early in your case to develop a strategy for valuing the business and making your case for how it should be treated in the division of property and debts.

12.27 My husband and I have owned and run our own business together for many years. Can I be forced out of it?

Maybe. Deciding what should happen with a family business when divorce occurs can be a challenge. Because of the risk for future conflict between divorcing spouses, the value of the business is likely to be substantially decreased if both remain owners, but this is not true for all businesses in all cases.

In discussing your options with your lawyer, consider the following questions:

- If one spouse retains ownership of the business, are there enough other assets for the other spouse to receive a fair share of the total marital assets?
- Which spouse has the skills and experience to continue running the business?
- What would you do if you weren't working in the business?
- What is the value of the business?
- What is the market for the business if it were to be sold?
- Could either spouse remain an employee of the business for some period of time even if not an owner?

You and your spouse know your business best. With the help of your lawyers, you may be able to create a settlement that can satisfy you both. If not, the judge will make the decision for you at trial.

12.28 I suspect my spouse is hiding assets, but I can't prove it. How can I protect myself if I discover later that I was right?

First, explore with your lawyer all the ways in which full disclosure might be achieved. If it just is not possible to find and prove everything necessary during the divorce, ask your lawyer to include language in your divorce decree to address your concern (sometimes called an "*Amie* clause"). Insist that it include an acknowledgment by your spouse that the agreement was based upon a full and complete disclosure of your spouse's financial condition, and the consequences if it is later proven that something was omitted. Discuss with your lawyer a provision that allows continuing jurisdiction over assets that are not disclosed.

12.29 My spouse says I'm not entitled to a share of his stock options because he gets to keep them only if he stays employed with his company. What are my rights?

Stock options are often very valuable assets. They are also a very complex issue when dividing assets during a divorce for these, among other, reasons:

- Each company has its own rules about awarding and exercising stock options.
- Complete information is needed from the employer.
- There are different methods for calculating the value of stock options, and Nevada law is fairly undeveloped as to which method should be used.
- The reasons the options were given can impact the valuation. For example, some are given for prior service, some for future performance, some are mixed, and for some there is no evidence either way.
- There are cost and tax considerations when options are exercised.

Rather than being awarded a portion of the stock options themselves, you are likely to receive a share of the proceeds when the stock options are exercised.

In Nevada, stock options are community property to the degree that they are considered—or ruled—to have been "acquired" during the marriage. Generally, they are considered an asset of the community when they are awarded, even if they have not yet vested, although conditions relating to continued, post-divorce employment may affect their "character" as separate property or community property assets, in part or entirely.

If either you or your spouse owns stock options, bring that asset to the attention of your lawyer early in your case to allow sufficient time to settle the issues or to be well prepared for trial.

12.30 What is a *prenuptial agreement* and how might it affect the property settlement phase of the divorce?

A *prenuptial agreement,* sometimes referred to as a *premarital* or *antenuptial agreement,* is a contract entered into between two people prior to their marriage. It can include provisions for how assets and debts will be divided in the event the marriage is terminated, as well as terms concerning alimony.

Your property settlement is likely to be greatly impacted by the terms of your prenuptial agreement if the agreement is upheld as valid by the court, because the very purpose of most such documents is to alter how property and debts will be distributed in the event of divorce.

12.31. Can a prenuptial agreement be contested during the divorce?

Yes. The court may consider many factors in determining whether to uphold your prenuptial agreement. Among them are:

- Whether your agreement was entered into voluntarily
- Whether your agreement was fair and reasonable at the time it was signed
- Whether you and your spouse gave a complete disclosure of your assets and debts

- Whether you and your spouse each had the opportunity to consult with independent counsel before signing the agreement
- Whether you and your spouse each had enough time to consider the agreement

If you have a prenuptial agreement, bring a copy of it to the initial consultation with your attorney. Be sure to provide your lawyer with a detailed history of the facts and circumstances surrounding reaching and signing the agreement.

12.32 I've heard the old saying, "Possession is nine tenths of the law." Is that true during divorce proceedings?

Not really. Nevada is a presumptive equal division community property state and it does not matter which spouse has possession of a community asset when the division of assets is being accomplished.

Consulting with an attorney before the filing of divorce can reduce the risk that assets will be hidden, transferred, or destroyed by your spouse. This is especially important if your spouse has a history of destroying property, waste, incurring substantial debt, or transferring money without your knowledge.

These are among the possible actions you and your attorney can consider together:

- Placing your family heirlooms or other valuables in a safe location
- Transferring some portion of financial accounts into secure one-party accounts prior to filing for divorce
- Preparing an inventory of the personal property
- Taking photographs or video of the property
- Obtaining copies of important records or statements
- Obtaining a JPI (joint preliminary injunction) and serving it with the complaint and summons for divorce

Plans to leave the marital home should also be discussed in detail with your attorney, so that any actions taken early in your case are consistent with your ultimate goals.

Speak candidly with your lawyer about your concerns so a plan can be developed that provides a level of protection that is appropriate to your circumstances.

12.33 I'm Jewish and want my husband to cooperate with obtaining a *get,* which is a divorce document under our religion. Can I get a court order for this?

Talk to your lawyer about obtaining a *get* cooperation clause in your divorce decree, including a provision regarding who should pay for it. At this time, the law regarding this has not been established in Nevada, and religious authorities have expressed different views on the validity of a get obtained by direction of the civil courts.

12.34 Who will get the frozen embryo of my egg and my spouse's sperm that we have stored at the health clinic?

The law on this issue is not yet established in Nevada. The terms of your contract with the clinic may impact the rights you and your spouse have to the embryo, so provide a copy of this contract to your attorney for review.

The potential resolutions include coming to an agreement as to disposition, or giving the power to decide what to do about the embryo to one spouse or the other. If permissible under your contract, you and your spouse may want to consider donating the embryo to another couple.

There are questions as to possible future support obligations for a child, and the law governing "artificial reproduction technology" is in considerable flux. You should discuss the subject with your lawyer and ensure that your lawyer is aware of all current developments in this rapidly changing area of the law.

12.35 Will debts be considered when determining the division of the property?

Yes. The court should consider the marital debts when dividing the property. For example, if you are awarded a car valued at $12,000, but you owe a $10,000 debt on the same vehicle, the court will take that debt into consideration in the overall division of the assets. Similarly, if one spouse agrees to pay substantial marital credit card debt, the obligation will also be considered in the final determination of the division of property and debts.

If your spouse incurred debts that you believe should be his or her sole responsibility, tell your attorney. Some debts may be considered nonmarital and treated separately from other debts incurred during the marriage. For example, if your spouse spent large sums of money on gambling or illegal drugs without your knowledge, you may be able to argue that those debts should be the sole responsibility of your spouse.

12.36 What happens to the property distribution if one of us dies before the divorce proceedings are completed?

If your spouse dies prior to your divorce decree being entered, normally the divorce action will "abate" (essentially, be canceled); you will be considered married and treated as a surviving spouse under the law.

If the only thing that was remaining in your divorce was the entry of the decree by the court, however, it can still be entered *nunc pro tunc* (meaning "now for then"), which would allow the court to effectively enter the decree before the death of your spouse, and so leave you divorced upon your spouse's death.

13

Benefits: Insurance, Retirement, and Pensions

During your marriage, you might have taken certain employment benefits for granted. You might not have given much thought each month to having insurance through your spouse's work. When you find yourself in a divorce, suddenly these benefits come to the forefront of your mind.

You might also, even unconsciously, have seen your own employment retirement benefits as belonging to you and not also to your spouse and referred to "my 401(k)" or "my pension." After all, you are the one who went to work every day to earn it, right?

When you divorce, some benefits to you arising from your spouse's employment will end, some may continue for a period of time, and others may be divided between you. Retirement funds, in particular, are often one of the most valuable marital assets to be divided in a divorce.

Whether the benefits are from your employment or from your spouse's, with your attorney's help you will develop a better understanding of which benefits the law considers to be "yours," "mine," and "ours" for continuing or dividing. Finally, upon divorce, you should amend your will and beneficiary designations to be sure they reflect your current reality and wishes, and to avoid unpleasant surprises later.

13.1 Will my children continue to have health coverage through my spouse's work even though we're divorcing?

If either you or your spouse currently provides health insurance for your children, it is very likely that the court will order the insurance to remain in place for so long as it remains available and support is being paid for your child.

The cost of insurance for the children should usually be taken into consideration in determining the amount of child support to be paid.

13.2 Will I continue to have health insurance through my spouse's work after the divorce?

It depends. If your spouse currently provides health insurance for you, you may usually be treated as a spouse for health insurance purposes for six months following the entry of your divorce decree. However, some insurance companies refuse to treat a person as a spouse beyond thirty days after the entry of the divorce decree.

Investigate the cost of continuing on your spouse's employer provided plans under a federal law known as *COBRA*. This coverage can usually be maintained for up to three years. However, the cost can be very high, so you will want to determine whether it's a realistic option.

Certain employers (the federal government, the state of Nevada, the military, etc.) have special rules and programs for insurance coverage. Each is different. Make sure you and your lawyer both know what benefits and options are available.

Tell your attorney if you want to be kept on your spouse's health insurance policy. If you have no other health insurance, this is an important provision to be included in your divorce decree.

Begin early to investigate your options for your future health insurance. The cost of your health care is an important factor when pursuing spousal support and planning your post-divorce budget.

The law governing health insurance is in rapid flux in the United States. Things could change quickly and significantly. Make sure your lawyer is aware of whatever options are available at the time of your divorce.

13.3 What is a QMCSO?

A *Qualified Medical Child Support Order (QMCSO)* is a court order providing continued group health insurance coverage for a minor child. A QMCSO may also enable a parent to obtain other information about the plan without having to go through the parent who has the coverage.

Rather than allowing only the parent with the insurance to be reimbursed for a claim, under a QMCSO, a health insurance plan is required to reimburse directly whoever actually paid the child's medical expense.

13.4 How many years must I have been married before I'm eligible to receive a part of my spouse's retirement fund or pension?

Even if your marriage is not of long duration, you may be entitled to a portion of your spouse's retirement fund or pension accumulated during the marriage. For example, if you were married for three years and your spouse contributed $10,000 to a 401(k) plan during the marriage, the starting presumption is that you are entitled to half of the value of that contribution when dividing your property and debts.

13.5 I contributed to my pension plan for ten years before I got married. Will my spouse get half of my entire pension?

Probably not. It is more likely the court will award your spouse only half of whatever portion of your retirement was acquired during the marriage.

If either you or your spouse made premarital contributions to a pension or retirement plan, be sure to let your attorney know. This information is essential to determine which portion of the retirement plan should be treated as "premarital" and thus unlikely to be shared.

13.6 I plan to keep my same job after my divorce. Will my former spouse get half of the money I contribute to my retirement plan after my divorce?

No, as long as no mistakes are made. Your former spouse should be entitled to only half of whatever portion of your retirement was acquired *during* the marriage.

There are different kinds of retirement plans. For "cash" plans, like 401(k) accounts, each spouse's portion can be separated out and put into its own account. For classic "pension" plans, such as a military retirement, that make payments every month after retirement, the share each spouse gets is determined by the "time rule." For details of the time rule, see the explanation in the article "Divorcing the Military: How to Attack and How to Defend," which is posted at http://willicklawgroup.com/military-retirement-benefits/.

Talk with your attorney so that the language of the divorce decree—and the language of any follow-up QDRO or other enforcement order, protects your post-divorce retirement contributions.

13.7 Am I still entitled to a share of my spouse's retirement even though I never contributed to one during our twenty-five-year marriage?

Probably. A retirement is often the most valuable asset accumulated during a marriage. Consequently, your judge should consider the retirement along with all of the other marital assets and debts when determining a fair division.

13.8 My lawyer says I'm entitled to a share of my spouse's retirement. How can I find out how much I get and when I'm eligible to receive it?

More than one factor will determine your right to collect from your spouse's retirement. One factor will be the terms of the court order dividing the retirement. The court order will tell you whether you are entitled to a set dollar amount, a percentage, or a fraction to be determined based upon the length of your marriage and how long your spouse continues working.

Another factor will be the terms of the retirement plan itself. Some provide for lump sum withdrawals; others issue payments in monthly installments, and only after the employee reaches a certain age. Review the terms of your court order and contact the plan administrator to obtain the clearest understanding of your rights and benefits.

For most kinds of retirement benefits, you need a special order in addition to your divorce decree to actually get any money from a spouse's retirement plan. This order should be obtained as close to the date of the divorce as possible. If it is not in place when your spouse retires, or dies, the absence of the order could stop you from collecting any benefits even if the divorce court ordered them to be paid.

You should also consult with a qualified pension division expert on drafting the proper Qualified Domestic Relations Order (QDRO). You can find such experts at www.qdromasters.com.

13.9 If I am eligible to receive my spouse's retirement benefits, do I have to be sixty-five to collect them?

It depends upon the terms of your spouse's retirement plan. In some cases it is possible to begin receiving your share at the earliest date your spouse is eligible to receive them, regardless of whether he or she elects to do so. Check the terms of your spouse's plan to learn your options.

13.10 What happens if my former spouse is old enough to receive benefits but I'm not?

Ordinarily you will be eligible to begin receiving your share of the benefits when your former spouse begins to receive his or hers. Depending upon the plan, you may be eligible to receive them sooner.

13.11 Am I entitled to cost-of-living increases on my share of my spouse's retirement?

It depends. If your spouse has a retirement plan that includes a provision for a *cost-of-living adjustment (COLA),* talk to your lawyer about whether this can be included in the court order dividing the retirement.

13.12 What circumstances might prevent me from getting part of my spouse's retirement benefits?

Some pension plans are not subject to direct division. If such plans were accrued during marriage, it is sometimes possible to compensate the nonemployee spouse by way of other assets. Other kinds of plans are not directly divisible, but require work-arounds, such as contractual redemption agreements or constructive trusts.

Sometimes there are restrictions on a former spouse's eligibility for certain kinds of benefits under a plan, such as remarriage restrictions to be eligible for survivor's benefits.

Make sure you and your lawyer know exactly what pension and retirement benefits are involved in your case, and obtain whatever additional expert assistance is necessary to fairly account for them in the property settlement of your case.

13.13 Does the death of my spouse affect the payout of retirement benefits to me or to our children?

It depends upon both the nature of your spouse's retirement plan and the terms of the court order dividing the retirement. Some plans allow only a surviving spouse or former spouse to be a beneficiary. Others may allow for the naming of an alternate beneficiary, such as your children.

Certain kinds of plans are divided in such a way that two separate interests are created—one for you, and one for your spouse—so that the death of either of you has no effect on the benefits payable to the other.

If you want to be eligible for survivorship benefits from your spouse's pension, discuss the issue with your attorney before your case is settled or goes to trial. If your attorney does not know enough about the plan to advise you, suggest retaining an expert who does.

13.14 How can I be sure I'll get my share of my former spouse's retirement when I am entitled to it years from now?

Rather than relying upon your former spouse to pay you a share of a future retirement, your best protection is a court order that provides for the retirement or pension plan administrator to pay the money directly to you. This type of court order is often referred to as a *Qualified Domestic Relations Order (QDRO)* or, in the case of federal retirement plans, a *Court Order Acceptable for Processing (COAP)*. Such orders help ensure that a nonemployee spouse receives his or her share directly from the employee spouse's plan.

Obtaining a QDRO or COAP is a critical step in the divorce process. They can be complex documents, and a number of steps are required to reduce future concerns about enforcement and fully protect your rights. These court orders must comply with numerous technical rules and be approved by the plan administrator, which is often located outside of Nevada.

Whenever possible, court orders dividing retirement plans should be entered at the same time as the decree of dissolution. Again, seek the assistance of a pension division expert. Visit www.qdromasters.com for more information on these experts and the division of retirement plans.

13.15 If my former spouse passes on before I do, can I still collect his or her Social Security benefits?

It depends. If you were married to your spouse for ten or more years and you have not remarried, you may be eligible for benefits. Contact your local Social Security Administration (SSA) office or visit the SSA website at www.ssa.gov.

13.16 What orders might the court enter regarding life insurance?

The judge may order you or your spouse to maintain a life insurance policy naming the other spouse, or the children, usually as security to ensure that future support payments are made. There are a lot of considerations, including who is to be the beneficiary (who gets how much from the policy), and who is to be the owner (who controls whether the policy can be changed, borrowed against, etc.)

In most cases you will be required to pay for your own life insurance after your divorce, and you should include this as an expense in your monthly budget.

13.17 Because we share children, should I consider my spouse as a beneficiary on my life insurance?

It depends on your intentions. If your intention is to give the money to your former spouse, by all means name the other parent as beneficiary.

However, if you intend the life insurance proceeds to be used for the benefit of your children, talk with your attorney about your options. You may consider naming a trustee to manage the life insurance proceeds on behalf of your children, and there may be reasons to choose someone other than your former spouse.

13.18 Can the court require in the decree that I be the beneficiary of my spouse's insurance policy, so long as the children are minors or indefinitely?

When a court order is entered for life insurance, it is ordinarily for the purposes of ensuring payment of future support and normally will terminate when the support obligation has ended. Currently, in Nevada law, there are few restrictions on the ability of a trial court to order maintenance of insurance, but you should discuss what options are available at the time of your divorce with your lawyer.

13.19 My spouse is in the military. What are my rights to benefits after the divorce?

As the former spouse of a military member, the types of benefits to which you may be entitled are typically determined by the number of years you were married, the number of years your spouse was in the military while you were married, and (for certain benefits) whether or not you remarry after divorce. Be sure you obtain accurate information about these dates.

Among the benefits for which you may be eligible are:

- A portion of your spouse's military retirement pay
- A survivor benefit in the event of your spouse's death
- Health care or participation in a temporary, transitional health care program
- Use of certain military facilities, such as the commissary

While your divorce is pending, educate yourself about your right to future military benefits so that you can plan for your future with clarity. A great deal of information, explaining all of these benefits in detail, along with information about eligibility and conditions, is posted at http://willicklawgroup.com/military-retirement-benefits/.

Contact a pension division expert before the divorce if possible to ensure you do not lose benefits due to an error in timing or poor language in your decree. Contact the experts at www.qdromasters.com to make sure you protect your benefits and rights.

13.20 Should I be concerned about my existing will or trust if I'm getting a divorce?

Absolutely. A will can be changed at any time and you should make sure you do so upon divorce. If you do not change your will and any trusts you may have (your "estate plan") your former spouse may end up remaining as the beneficiary of your estate, even if you do not wish that to happen.

You may not be allowed to change your estate plan during the divorce process. Local rules in some counties prohibit changing any beneficiary designations during a divorce case. Even if you can do so, any changes made to your estate plan during the divorce process may not be effective as to your spouse's share of community property.

But you should definitely amend your will to reflect your intended beneficiaries as soon as possible after the divorce. If possible, have a new will prepared during the divorce action and sign it the same day as the divorce is granted, or as soon afterwards as you can. Many stories exist about people who "intended" to change their will after a divorce, but die in accidents before they get around to it—leaving their old will in place, with their former spouse as beneficiary.

Such "old wills" are sometimes challenged by the intended beneficiaries (usually, other family members or new spouses) in probate, but this is only successful sometimes, and the cost is very high in both money and emotional strain. It is far better, for everyone, to simply execute a new will (or trust) immediately after your divorce.

Trusts are even more complicated; some are irrevocable, but most "family trusts" can and should be "unwound" either during the divorce process (if permitted) or immediately afterward.

If your divorce attorney is not well versed in estate planning, wills, trusts, and probate, you should seek the counsel of an attorney that specializes in this area of the law. Feel free to ask your divorce lawyer for a referral.

13.21 If I don't change the beneficiary on my life insurance policy and my retirement plan, can I direct who gets the benefits in the divorce decree or my will?

No. Unfortunately, the law does not require insurance companies or retirement plans to recognize a change in beneficiary that was not made through the plan or company directly. In fact, even a court order that requires an insured to change the beneficiary, or a divorce decree in which your former spouse gives up all interest in your retirement plan, is not binding on the company or plan unless they were specifically "joined" in the divorce action and have participated in the action before the court (and in Nevada, this is almost never done).

What you are required to do is obtain a "beneficiary change form" from each retirement plan or insurance policy you have, and specifically direct the plan or policy to remove your former spouse as your named beneficiary. If you fail to do this, your former spouse will probably be paid the insurance or survivorship benefits if you die, even if you do not want this to happen.

If your divorce lawyer is not well versed in retirement and survivorship benefits, and you need any assistance dealing with changing your survivorship designations, ask your lawyer for a referral to an attorney who does know about such things.

14

Division of Debts

Throughout a marriage, most couples will have disagreements about money from time to time. You might think extra money should be spent on a family vacation, but your spouse insists it should be saved for your retirement. You might think it's time to finally buy a new car, but your spouse thinks your driving the ten-year-old van for two more years is a better idea.

If you and your spouse had different philosophies about saving and spending during your marriage, chances are you will have some differing opinions when dividing your debts in divorce. What you both can count on is that Nevada law provides that, to reach a fair outcome, the payment of debts must also be taken into consideration when dividing the assets from your marriage.

There are steps you can take to ensure the best outcome possible when it comes to dividing your marital debt. These include providing accurate and complete debt information to your lawyer and asking your lawyer to include provisions in your divorce decree to protect you in the future if your spouse refuses to pay his or her share.

Regardless of how the debts from your marriage are divided, know that you will gradually build your independent financial security when making a fresh start after your divorce is final.

14.1 Who is responsible for paying credit card bills and making house payments during the divorce proceedings?

In most cases, the court will not make decisions regarding the payment of credit card debt on a temporary basis unless the parties force the issue into court during pre-divorce proceedings. Work with your attorney and your spouse to reach a temporary agreement if at all possible. Discuss the importance of making at least minimum payments on time to avoid substantial finance charges and late fees.

Typically, the spouse who remains in the home will be responsible for the mortgage payments, taxes, utilities, and most other ordinary expenses. But it depends on that party's ability to make the payments. Most courts will address those responsibilities early on in the divorce process if the parties have not reached an agreement.

If you are concerned that you cannot afford to stay in the marital home on a temporary basis, talk with your attorney about your options prior to your temporary hearing.

14.2 What, if anything, should I be doing with the credit card companies as we go through the divorce?

If possible, it is best to obtain some separate credit prior to the divorce. This will help you establish credit in your own name and help you with necessary purchases following a separation.

Begin by obtaining a copy of your credit report from at least two of the three nationwide consumer reporting companies: Experian, Equifax, or TransUnion. The Fair Credit Reporting Act entitles you to a free copy of your credit report from each of these three companies every twelve months.

To order your free annual report online, go to www.annualcreditreport.com, call toll free to (877) 322-8228, or complete an Annual Credit Report Request Form and mail it to: Annual Credit Report Request Service, P.O. Box 105281, Atlanta, Georgia 30348-5281. You can print the form from the Federal Trade Commission website at www.ftc.gov/credit.

These are free resources. Many companies ask you to pay them to obtain these reports for you. Ignore such offers—they are scams.

Your spouse may have incurred debt using your name. This information is important to relay to your attorney. If you and your spouse have joint credit card accounts, contact each credit card company to remove your name from your spouse's accounts, remove your spouse as an authorized user on each of your accounts, or close the accounts.

If you want to maintain credit with a company, ask to have a new account in your own name. Be sure to let your spouse know if you close an account he or she has been using.

14.3 How is credit card debt divided?

Credit card debt will be divided as a part of the overall division of the marital property and debts. Just as in the division of property, the court considers what is equitable, or fair, in your case. Nevada law starts with an equal division of community property, and most courts consider the marital debt to be on the same balance sheet.

If your spouse has exclusively used a credit card for purposes that did not benefit the family, such as gambling, talk with your attorney. In most cases the court will not review a lengthy history of how you and your spouse used the credit cards, but there can be exceptions.

14.4 Am I responsible for repayment of my spouse's student loans?

It depends. If your spouse incurred student loans prior to the marriage, it is most likely that he or she will be ordered to pay that debt.

If the debt was incurred during the marriage, how the funds were used may have an impact on who is ordered to pay them. For example, if your spouse borrowed $3,000 during the marriage for tuition, it is likely your spouse will be ordered to pay that debt. However, if a $3,000 student loan was taken out by your spouse, but $1,000 of it was used for a family vacation, then the court would be more likely to order the debt shared.

The court may also look at whether the community benefitted from the additional education. If so, you may have to assist with the repayment.

The court may also consider payment on student loan debt when calculating the amount of spousal support to be paid.

If you were a joint borrower on your spouse's student loan and your spouse fails to pay the loan, the lender may attempt to collect from you even if your spouse has been ordered to pay the debt.

If either you or your spouse has student loan debt, be sure to give your attorney the complete history regarding the debt and ask about the most likely outcome under the facts of your case.

14.5 During the divorce proceedings, am I still responsible for debt my spouse continues to accrue?

It depends. In most cases the court will order each of the parties to be responsible for his or her own post-separation debts. But in the absence of an agreement, or temporary order, the court may consider debts accrued during separation as part of the debt to be divided upon divorce.

During separation, if debts were incurred for necessary expenses by one spouse because the other spouse with most or all of the income was not sharing that income, it is common for the court to consider the debt marital.

14.6 During the marriage my spouse applied for and received several credit cards without my knowledge. Am I responsible for them?

It depends. The court will consider the overall fairness of the property and debt division when deciding who should pay that debt. If your spouse bought items with the cards and intends to keep those items, it is likely that your spouse will be ordered to pay the debt incurred for the purchases. How long such an arrangement has been in place, and whether it appears that both parties agreed to it could be relevant.

The credit card companies are unlikely to be able to pursue collection from you for the debt unless your spouse used them for the necessities of life, such as food, necessary clothing, or housing.

In any event, you should always bring the existence of such credit cards to the attention of your lawyer to deal with the matter during the divorce proceedings.

14.7 During our marriage, we paid off thousands of dollars of debt incurred by my spouse before we were married. Will the court take this into consideration when dividing our property and debt?

It might. Just as premarital assets can have an impact on the overall division of property and debts, so can premarital debt. Depending upon the length of the marriage, the evidence of the debt, and the amount paid, it may be a factor for the judge to consider.

Be sure to let your attorney know if either you or your spouse brought substantial debt into the marriage, and what happened to that debt during the marriage.

14.8 Regarding debts, what is a *hold-harmless clause,* and why should it be in the divorce decree?

A *hold-harmless* provision is intended to protect you in the event that your spouse fails to follow a court order to pay a debt after the divorce is granted. The language typically provides that your spouse shall "indemnify and hold [you] harmless from liability" on the debt.

If you and your spouse have a joint debt and your spouse fails to pay, the creditor may nevertheless attempt to collect from you. This is because the court is without power to change the creditor's rights and can make orders affecting only you and your spouse.

In the event your spouse fails to pay a court-ordered debt and the creditor attempts collection from you, the "hold-harmless" provision in your divorce decree can be used in an effort to insist that payment is made by your former spouse, either to the creditor, or to reimburse you for any sums you have to pay the creditor.

14.9 Why do my former spouse's doctors say they have a legal right to collect from me when my former spouse was ordered to pay her own medical bills?

Under Nevada law, you might be held liable for the "necessities of life" of your spouse, such as health care. Your divorce decree does not take away the legal rights of creditors to collect certain debts, especially when both parties signed for the credit or debt.

There are several things that could lead to this situation, and several different ways it could play out, depending on who actually signed for what, when the debt was incurred, what the divorce decree provides, and the actual abilities of the parties to potentially pay the debt. Contact your attorney about your rights to enforce the court order that your spouse pay his or her own medical bills.

14.10 My spouse and I have agreed that I will keep our home; why must I refinance the mortgage?

There may be a number of reasons why your spouse is asking you to refinance the mortgage.

First, the mortgage company cannot be forced to take your spouse's name off the mortgage note. This means that if you did not make the house payments, the lender could pursue collection against your spouse.

Second, your spouse may not want to wait to receive a share of the home equity. It may be possible for you to borrow additional money at the time of refinancing to pay your spouse his or her share of the equity in the home.

Third, the mortgage on your family home may prevent your spouse from buying a home in the future, at least for a specific period of time, even if you are making the payments on the former home. Because there remains a risk that your spouse could be pursued for the debt to the mortgage company, a second lender may not wish to take the risk of extending further credit to your spouse.

14.11 Can I file for bankruptcy while my divorce is pending?

Yes. Consult with your attorney if you are considering filing for bankruptcy while your divorce is pending. It will be important for you to ask yourself a number of questions, such as:

- Should I file for bankruptcy on my own or with my spouse?
- How will filing for bankruptcy affect my ability to purchase a home in the future?
- Which debts can be discharged in bankruptcy, and which cannot?
- How will a bankruptcy affect the division of property and debts in the divorce?
- How might a delay in the divorce proceeding due to a bankruptcy impact my case?
- What form of bankruptcy is best for my situation?

If you use a different attorney for your bankruptcy than you have for your divorce, be sure that each attorney is kept fully informed about the developments in the other case.

14.12 What happens if my spouse files for bankruptcy during our divorce?

Contact your attorney right away. The filing of a bankruptcy while your divorce is pending can have a significant impact on your divorce. Your attorney can advise you whether certain debts are likely to be discharged in the bankruptcy, the delay a bankruptcy may cause to your divorce, and what impact the bankruptcy might have on the distribution of property and debts, and any support claims, in your divorce case. You should also ask, depending on the circumstances, whether bankruptcy is an appropriate option for you as well.

14.13 Can I file for divorce while I am in bankruptcy?

Yes, however, you must receive the bankruptcy court's permission to proceed with some aspects of the divorce. While in bankruptcy, your property is protected from debt collection by the *automatic stay*. The stay can also prevent the divorce court from dividing property between you and your spouse until you obtain the bankruptcy court's permission to proceed with the divorce.

The full interplay of divorce and bankruptcy law is extremely complicated, and it changes from time to time. You should fully explore all impacts of a bankruptcy upon your divorce with both your bankruptcy and divorce lawyers.

14.14 What should I do if my former spouse files for bankruptcy after our divorce?

Contact your attorney immediately. If you learn that your former spouse has filed for bankruptcy, you may have certain rights to object to the discharge of any debts your spouse was ordered to pay under your divorce decree, but your time to do so may be limited. If you fail to take action quickly, it is possible that you will be held responsible for debts your spouse was ordered to pay, or you could suffer other economic harm.

15

Taxes

Nobody wants to receive a surprise letter from the Internal Revenue Service saying he or she owes more taxes. When your divorce is over, you want to be sure that you don't later discover you owe taxes you weren't expecting to pay.

A number of tax issues may arise in your divorce. Your attorney may not be able to answer all of your tax questions, so consulting your accountant or tax advisor for additional advice might be necessary.

Taxes are important considerations in both settlement negotiations and trial preparation. They should not be overlooked. Taxes can impact many of your decisions, including those regarding alimony, division of property, and the receipt of benefits.

Perhaps more so than in any other area of law, tax law changes constantly. Everything said here should be checked with your lawyer and tax advisor, to be sure it is still correct and current at the time of your divorce.

15.1 Will either my spouse or I have to pay income tax when we transfer property or pay a property settlement to one another according to our divorce decree?

No. However, it is important that you see the future tax consequences of a subsequent withdrawal, sale, or transfer of certain assets you receive in your divorce. At the very least, be aware of the difference in value between "pretax" assets and "posttax" assets, and be wary about trading one for the other.

It is important to ask your attorney to take tax consequences into consideration when looking at the division of your assets. You should be sure you understand the actual meaning of the terms being used, and the values of the assets being distributed.

15.2 Is the amount of child support I pay tax deductible?

No.

15.3 Do I have to pay income tax on any child support I receive?

No. Your child support is tax-free regardless of when it is paid or when it is received.

15.4 Is the amount of alimony I am ordered to pay tax deductible?

Probably. Spousal support paid pursuant to a court order is normally deductible, *unless* the court specifies in the order that it is *not* to be tax deductible. This will include court-ordered alimony and may also include other forms of support provided to your former spouse (but not child support).

Your tax deduction is a factor to consider when determining a fair amount of alimony to be paid in your case, and normally deserves a full discussion with your tax advisor before entering into any agreements or proceeding to trial.

15.5 Do I have to pay tax on the alimony I receive?

Probably. You must pay income tax on the spousal support you receive, *unless* the court specifies in the order that it is *not* to be tax includable. This will include court-ordered alimony and may also include other forms of spousal support, but not child support, paid by your spouse.

Income tax is a critical factor in determining a fair amount of alimony. If there is a difference in post-divorce tax rates between the parties, it is possible in many cases to increase the amount received by the alimony recipient while not increasing the amount spent by the obligor. Insist that your attorney bring this issue to the attention of your spouse's lawyer, or to the judge, if your case proceeds to trial, so that both the tax you pay and the deduction your spouse receives are taken into consideration.

Be sure to consult with your tax advisor about payment of tax on your spousal support. Making estimated tax payments throughout the year or withholding additional taxes from your wages can avoid a burdensome tax liability at the end of the year. Tax law changes constantly, so be sure to get updated advice from your tax advisor before settlement or trial.

It is important to budget for payment of tax on your alimony. Taxes are also another item to consider when looking at your monthly living expenses for the purposes of seeking an alimony award.

15.6 During the divorce proceedings, is our tax filing status affected?

It can be. You are considered unmarried if your decree is final by December 31 of the tax year.

If you are considered unmarried, your filing status is either "single" or, under certain circumstances, "head of household." If your decree is not final as of December 31, your filing status is either "married filing a joint return" or "married filing a separate return," unless you live apart from your spouse and meet the exception for "head of household."

While your divorce is in progress, talk to both your tax advisor and your attorney about your filing status. It may be beneficial to figure your tax on both a joint return and a separate return to see which gives you the lower tax. IRS Publication 504, Divorced or Separated Individuals, provides more detail on tax issues while you are going through a divorce.

15.7 Should I file a joint income tax return with my spouse while our divorce is pending?

Consult your tax advisor to determine the risks and benefits of filing a joint return with your spouse. Compare this with the consequences of filing your tax return separately. Often, the overall tax liability will be less with the filing of a joint return, but there are other considerations, including any concerns you have about the accuracy and truthfulness of the information on the tax return.

If you have any doubts, consult both your attorney and your tax advisor before agreeing to sign a joint tax return with your spouse.

Prior to filing a return with your spouse, try to reach agreement about how any tax owed or refund expected will be shared, and ask your lawyer to assist you in getting this in writing, to avoid future disputes.

15.8 For tax purposes, is one time of year better to divorce than another?

It depends upon your tax situation. If you and your spouse agree that it would be beneficial to file joint tax returns for the year in which you are divorcing, you may wish to not have your divorce finalized before the end of the year.

Your marital status for filing income taxes is determined by your marital status on December 31.

15.9 What tax consequences should I consider regarding the sale of our home?

When your home is sold, whether during your divorce or after, the sale may be subject to a capital gains tax. Under recent rules, if your home was your primary residence and you lived in the home for two of the preceding five years, you may be eligible to exclude up to $250,000 of the gain on the sale of your home. If both you and your spouse meet the ownership and residence tests, you may be eligible to exclude up to $500,000 of the gain. These rules are subject to change at any time.

If you anticipate the gain on the sale of your residence to be over $250,000, talk with your attorney early in the divorce process about a plan to minimize the tax liability. For more information, see IRS Publication 523, Selling Your Home, or visit the IRS website at www.irs.gov and talk with your tax advisor.

15.10 How might capital gains tax be a problem for me years after the divorce?

Future capital gains tax on the sale of property should be discussed with your attorney during the negotiation and trial preparation stages of your case. This is especially important if the sale of the property is imminent. Failure to do so may result in an unfair outcome.

For example, suppose you agree that your spouse will be awarded the proceeds from the sale of your home valued at $200,000, after the real estate commission, and you will take the stock portfolio also valued at $200,000.

Suppose that, after the divorce, you decide to sell the stock. It is still valued at $200,000, but you learn that its original price was $120,000 and that you must pay capital gains tax of 15 percent on the $80,000 of gain. You pay tax of $12,000, leaving you with $188,000.

Meanwhile, your former spouse sells the marital home but pays no capital gains tax because he qualifies for the $250,000 exemption. He is left with the full $200,000.

There are untold variations on this theme—taxes matter in the value of assets distributed upon divorce. Tax implications of your property division should always be discussed with your attorney, with support from your tax advisor as needed.

15.11 During and after the divorce, who gets to claim the children as dependents?

This issue should be addressed in settlement negotiations or at trial, if settlement is not reached.

In Nevada, under current law, the judge has discretion to determine which parent will be entitled to claim the children as exemptions for income tax purposes.

If one party has income so low or so high that he or she will not benefit from the dependency exemption, the court may award the exemption to the other parent. It might make sense to trade the dependency exemptions to the other parent for additional support or property.

15.12 My decree says I have to sign IRS Form 8332 so my former spouse can claim our child as an exemption, since I have custody. Should I sign it once for all future years?

Probably not. Child custody and child support can be modified in the future. If there is a future modification of custody or support, which parent is entitled to claim your child as an exemption could change. The best practice is to provide your former spouse a timely copy of Form 8332 signed by you for the appropriate tax year only, one year at a time, if still called for.

15.13 Can my spouse and I split the child-care tax credit?

Only if you have more than one child needing child-care. Each parent can claim the credit for one of the children.

15.14 Is the cost of getting a divorce, including my attorney fees, tax deductible under any circumstances?

Your legal fees for getting a divorce are not deductible. However, a portion of your attorney fees may be deductible if they are for:

- The collection of sums included in your gross income, such as alimony or interest income
- Advice regarding the determination of taxes or tax due

Attorney's fees are "miscellaneous" deductions for individuals and are consequently limited to 2 percent of your adjusted gross income. More details can be found in IRS Publication 529, Miscellaneous Deductions.

You may also be able to deduct fees you pay to appraisers or accountants who help during your divorce. Talk to your tax advisor about whether any portion of your attorney's fees or other expenses from your divorce are deductible.

15.15 Do I have to complete a new Form W-4 for my employer because of my divorce?

Completing a new Form W-4, Employee's Withholding Certificate, will help you to claim the proper withholding allowances based upon your marital status and exemptions. Also, if you are receiving alimony, you may need to make quarterly estimated tax payments. Consult with your tax advisor to ensure you are making the most preferable tax planning decision.

15.16 What is *innocent spouse relief* and how can it help me?

Innocent spouse relief refers to a method of obtaining relief from the Internal Revenue Service for taxes otherwise owed by you and your spouse as a result of a joint income tax return filed during your marriage. Numerous factors affect your eligibility for innocent spouse tax relief, such as:

- You would suffer a financial hardship if you were required to pay the tax.
- You did not significantly benefit from the unpaid taxes.
- You suffered abuse during your marriage.
- You thought your spouse would pay the taxes on the original return.

Talk with your attorney and your tax advisor if you are concerned about liability for taxes arising from joint tax returns filed during the marriage. You may benefit from a referral to an attorney who specializes in tax law.

16

Filing Papers and Going to Court

For many of us, our images of going to court are created by movie scenes and our favorite television shows. We picture the witness breaking down in tears after a grueling cross-examination. We see lawyers strutting around the courtroom, waving their arms as they plead their case to the jury.

Hollywood drama, however, is a far cry from the usual reality. Going to court for your divorce can mean many things, ranging from sitting in a hallway while waiting for the lawyers and judges to conclude a conference, to being on the witness stand giving mundane answers to questions about your monthly living expenses.

Regardless of the nature of your court proceeding, going to court often evokes a sense of anxiety. Perhaps your divorce might be the first time in your life that you have even been in a courtroom. Be assured that those feelings of nervousness and uncertainty are normal.

Understanding what will occur in court and being well prepared for any court hearings will relieve much of your stress. Knowing the order of events, courtroom etiquette, the role of the people in the courtroom, and what is expected of you will make the entire experience easier.

Your lawyer will be with you at all times to support you any time you go to court. Remember, every court appearance moves you one step closer to completing your divorce so that you can move forward with your life.

16.1 I have heard that Nevada requires all court documents to be filed electronically. Is this true?

More and more so, yes. It varies by county, and at the time this book went to print, there was no uniformity, but rules about electronic filing, or "e-filing," are changing quickly. The court systems are trying to automate to reduce the amount of paper the court has to deal with, and lower costs. In some counties, all documents must be filed electronically with the court.

If you have an attorney, he or she will ensure that your documents are properly filed with the court. If you are representing yourself (i.e, acting in "proper person"), you will have to go to the court to file your documents or register with the court for an electronic filing account.

16.2 Is there any added cost for electronic filing?

This also varies from county to county throughout Nevada. If your attorney has an electronic filing account, there is probably a minimal fee associated with filing every document, or a fee is charged to the lawyer's office monthly or annually. If you are filing the documents on your own at the courthouse, there is no cost in most places, but be prepared to wait in long lines to accomplish the filing. Talk to your attorney about any additional costs associated with filing your documents beyond the filing fees.

16.3 What do I need to know about appearing in court and court dates in general?

Court dates are important. As soon as you receive a notice from your attorney about a court date in your case, confirm whether your attendance will be required and mark the date on your calendar.

Ask your attorney about the nature of the hearing, including whether the judge will be listening to testimony by witnesses, reading affidavits, or merely listening to the arguments of the lawyers.

Ask whether it is necessary for you to meet with your attorney or take any other action to prepare for the hearing, such as providing additional information or documents.

Find out how long the hearing is expected to last. It may be as short as a few minutes or as long as a day or more.

If you plan to attend the hearing, determine where and when to meet your attorney. Depending upon the type of hearing, your lawyer may want you to arrive in advance of the scheduled hearing time to prepare.

Make sure you know the location of the courthouse, where to park, and the floor and room number of the courtroom. Planning for such simple matters as having change available for a parking meter can eliminate unnecessary stress. If you want someone to go to court with you to provide you support, check with your attorney first.

16.4 When and how often will I need to go to court?

Whether and how often you will need to go to court depends upon a number of factors. Depending upon the complexity of your case and the degree to which it is contested, you may never actually have to go to the courthouse, or may have only one hearing, or may have numerous court hearings throughout the course of your divorce.

Some hearings, usually those on procedural matters, are attended only by the attorneys. These could include requests for the other side to provide information or for the setting of certain deadlines. These hearings are often brief. Other hearings, such as temporary hearings for custody or support, are typically attended by both parties and their attorneys.

If you and your spouse settle all of the issues in your case, the case might be "submitted on the papers" (i.e., there will be no hearing at all), or there could be a short "prove up" hearing. Either or both spouses, depending upon your situation, will be required to attend such a hearing. If you are the plaintiff, the spouse who filed the divorce complaint, plan to attend the final "prove up" hearing.

If your case proceeds to trial, your appearance will be required for the duration of the trial. In Nevada, divorce matters are heard before a judge only; juries do not hear divorces.

16.5 How much notice will I receive about appearing in court?

The amount of notice you will receive for any court hearing can vary from a few days to several weeks or longer. Ask your attorney whether and when it will be necessary for you to appear in court on your case so that you can have time to prepare and plan.

If you receive a notice of a hearing, contact your attorney immediately. He or she can tell you whether your appearance is required and what other steps are needed to prepare.

16.6 I am afraid to be alone in the same room with my spouse. When I go to court, is this going to happen if the lawyers go into the judge's office to discuss the case?

No. There should always be a court marshal or bailiff and a court clerk in the courtroom. If you have a concern, ensure your lawyer knows about it; he or she will ensure others remain present at all times.

16.7 Do I have to go to court every time a motion is filed?

Not necessarily. Some matters are decided "on the papers" without any appearances in court at all. Other matters will be decided by the judge after listening to the arguments of the lawyers without the need for your appearance. Check with your lawyer to see if you need to attend.

16.8 My spouse's lawyer keeps asking for continuances of court dates. Is there anything I can do to stop this?

Continuances of court dates are not unusual in divorces (or other legal matters). A court date might be postponed for many reasons, including a conflict on the calendar of one of the attorneys or the judge, the lack of availability of one of the parties or an important witness, or the need for more time to prepare.

Discuss with your attorney your desire to move your case forward without further delay, so that repeated requests for continuances can be vigorously resisted.

16.9 If I have to go to court, will I be put on the stand? Will there be a jury?

In Nevada, divorce matters are heard before a judge only; juries do not hear divorces. Whether you will be put on the stand to testify will depend upon the nature of the issues in dispute, the judge assigned to your case, and your attorney's strategy for your case.

16.10 My lawyer said I need to be in court for our *temporary orders hearing* next week. What's going to happen?

A *temporary orders hearing* is held to determine such matters as who remains in the house while your divorce is pending, temporary custody, and temporary support.

The procedure for your temporary hearing can vary depending upon the county in which your case was filed, the judge to which the case is assigned, and whether temporary custody is disputed.

Most temporary hearings are held on the basis of written affidavits/declarations and the arguments of the lawyers. You should plan to attend your temporary order hearing if possible, but you probably will not be asked to say or do anything during the hearing. However, your attorney may need additional information from you during the hearing, and last-minute negotiations to resolve temporary issues are not uncommon.

In some counties, your hearing will be one of numerous other hearings on the judge's calendar. You may find yourself in a courtroom with many other lawyers and their clients, all having matters scheduled before the court that day.

If temporary custody is disputed, you and other witnesses might be required to take the witness stand to give testimony at your temporary hearing. If this is the case, meeting with your attorney in advance to fully prepare is very important. Normally, your lawyer will know in advance if there is any possibility that you will be called on to give testimony during a hearing.

Talk to your lawyer about the procedure you should expect for the temporary hearing in your case.

16.11 Do I have to go to court if all of the issues in my case are settled?

Not necessarily. Check with your attorney to see if your presence is required. Sometimes, no one has to attend, and paperwork is simply prepared and submitted instead.

16.12 Are there any rules about courtroom etiquette that I need to know?

Knowing a few tips about being in the courtroom will make your experience easier.

- Dress appropriately. Avoid overly casual dress, lots of jewelry, revealing clothing, and extreme hairstyles. Generally, "slogan" T-shirts of any variety are a bad idea. If you are unclear about appropriate attire, consult your attorney in advance.
- Don't bring beverages—other than water—into the courtroom. Most courts have rules which do not allow food and drink in courtrooms.
- Dispose of chewing gum before entering the courtroom.
- Don't talk aloud in the courtroom unless you're on the witness stand or being questioned by the judge.
- Do not react to anything said by anyone who is not asking you a direct question. Don't exclaim disagreement, nod or shake your head, make hand gestures, fold your arms, or otherwise react. Behave at all times as if you are being judged on your appearance and behavior, because, at some level, you are.
- Stand up whenever the judge is entering or leaving the courtroom.
- Be sure to turn off your cell phone.

Although you may feel anxious initially, you'll likely feel more relaxed about the courtroom setting once your hearing gets underway.

16.13 What is the role of the *court marshal* or *bailiff*?

The *court marshal* or *bailiff* provides support and security for the judge, the lawyers, and the litigants in the management of the court calendar and the courtroom. He or she may assist in the scheduling of court hearing, the calling of witnesses or cases, and the management of legal documents given to the judge for review, such as temporary orders and divorce decrees. He or she is also responsible for the safety of all parties and the judge.

16.14 Will there be a *court reporter*, and what will he or she do?

A *court reporter* is a professional trained to make an accurate record of the words spoken and documents offered into evidence during court proceedings. Most counties in Nevada do not automatically have a court reporter in the family court rooms. Some counties use tape-or video-recording devices rather than court reporters, with a record available to the attorneys shortly after the hearing.

16.15 Will I be able to talk to my attorney while we are in court?

During court proceedings it is important that your attorney give his or her full attention to anything being said by the judge, witnesses, or your spouse's lawyer. For this reason, your attorney will usually avoid talking with you when anyone else in the courtroom is speaking.

It is critical that your attorney hear each question asked by the other lawyer and all answers given by each witness. If not, opportunities for making objections to inappropriate evidence may be lost. You can support your attorney in doing an effective job for you by avoiding talking to him or her while a court hearing is in progress.

Plan to have pen and paper with you when you go to court. If your court proceeding is underway and your lawyer is listening to what is being said by others in the courtroom, it is best to write him or her a note with any questions or comments.

If your court hearing is lengthy, breaks will be taken. You can use this time to discuss with your attorney any questions or observations you have about the proceeding.

16.16 What questions might my lawyer ask me at the final hearing about the problems in our marriage and why I want the divorce?

Because Nevada is a no-fault state, your lawyer will ask you questions to show the court that the parties are incompatible in marriage, without going into detail about the specific difficulties in your marriage.

The questions will be similar to these:

Attorney: Is it true that since the time of your marriage, your likes and dislikes, interests, and friends have grown separate and apart so that it is no longer possible for you to live together harmoniously as husband and wife?

You: Yes.

Attorney: Is there any possibility for a reconciliation?

You: No.

If your spouse disagrees, he or she may give the opinion that the marriage can be saved. However, most judges recognize that it takes two willing partners for a marriage to be reconciled. Effectively, Nevada is a "one party consent" state —if either of you wishes the marriage to end, a divorce will be granted.

It is unlikely that you will be asked in any detail about the nature of the marital problems that led to the divorce. In the majority of cases, questions like those above will satisfy the judge that the requirements under Nevada law for the dissolving of a marriage have been met.

16.17 My lawyer said that the judge has issued a *pretrial order* having to do with my upcoming trial and that we'll have to "comply" with it. What does this mean?

A *pretrial order* is issued by some judges to order that certain information be provided either to the opposing party or to the judge in advance of trial. This might include:

- A list of issues that have been settled

- A list of issues that are still disputed
- Agreements, referred to as *stipulations,* as to the truth of certain facts
- The names of witnesses
- A list (and copy) of exhibits
- A summary of how you want the judge to decide the case
- Deadlines for providing information

16.18. What is a *pretrial conference*?

A *pretrial conference* is a meeting held with the lawyers and the judge to review information related to an upcoming trial, such as:

- How long the trial is expected to last
- The issues in dispute
- The law surrounding the disputed issues
- The identification of witnesses
- Trial exhibits, and any stipulations for their admission
- The status of negotiations

Often, the trial date is set at the pretrial conference. If a pretrial conference is held in your case, ask your attorney whether you should attend. Your attorney may request that you either be present for the conference or be available by phone.

16.19 Besides meeting with my lawyer, is there anything else I should do to prepare for my upcoming trial?

Yes. Be sure to review your deposition (if one was taken) and any information you provided in your discovery, such as answers to interrogatories. At trial, it is possible that you will be asked some of the same questions. If you think you might give different answers at trial, discuss this with your lawyer.

It is important that your attorney know in advance of trial whether any information you provided during the discovery process has changed.

16.20 I'm meeting with my lawyer to prepare for trial. How do I make the most of these meetings?

Meeting with your lawyer to prepare for your trial is important to achieving a good outcome. Come to the meeting prepared to discuss the following:

- The issues in your case
- Your desired outcome on each of the issues
- The questions you might be asked at trial by both lawyers
- The exhibits that will be offered into evidence during the trial
- The witnesses for your trial
- The status of negotiations
- Any information that has changed since the time it was turned over to or discussed with your lawyer —employment, income, assets, debts, statements by children, etc.

Your meeting with your lawyer will help you better understand what to expect at your trial and make the trial experience easier.

16.21 My lawyer says that the law firm is busy with *trial preparation*. What exactly is my lawyer doing to prepare for my trial?

Countless tasks are necessary to perform to prepare your case for trial. These are just some of them:

- Developing arguments to be made on each of the contested issues. Outlining them, in writing, to provide a road map for the lawyer at the hearing
- Researching and reviewing the relevant law in your case
- Reviewing the facts of your case to determine which witnesses are best suited to testifying about them
- Reviewing, selecting, and preparing exhibits, and ensuring all necessary copies are delivered by the due date to opposing counsel and to the court
- Preparing questions for all witnesses

- Preparing an opening statement
- Reviewing rules of evidence to prepare for any objections expected to be made or opposed at trial
- Determining the order of witnesses and all exhibits
- Preparing your file for the day in court, including preparing a trial notebook with essential information

Your lawyer is committed to a good outcome for you in your divorce. He or she will be engaged in many important actions to fully prepare your case for trial.

16.22 My divorce is scheduled for trial. Does this mean there is no hope for a settlement?

Not necessarily. Many cases are settled after a trial date is set. The setting of a trial date may cause you and your spouse to think about the risks and costs of going to trial. This can help you and your spouse focus on what is most important to you and lead you toward a negotiated settlement.

Because the costs of preparing for and proceeding to trial are substantial, it is best to engage in settlement negotiations as far in advance of your trial date as possible; despite this reality, there are many cases that actually settle at the last possible moment—sometimes the day before trial, or even once trial has begun.

16.23 Can I prevent my spouse from being in the courtroom?

Probably not. Because your spouse has a legal interest in the outcome of your divorce, he or she has a right to be present, just as you do. As a general rule, Nevada courtrooms are open to the public. If you desire a closed hearing, make sure that you inform your lawyer of that request.

16.24 Can I take a friend or family member with me to court?

Yes. Let your attorney know in advance if you intend to bring anyone to court with you. Some people important to you may be very emotional about your divorce or your spouse. Be sure to invite someone who is better able to focus attention on supporting you rather than on his or her own feelings. Also, if the other person is a witness, they may be excluded until called to testify.

Once a witness has completed his or her testimony, he or she will ordinarily be allowed to remain in the courtroom for the remainder of the trial.

Talk to your attorney about who it is you would like to bring into the courtroom, and what the relevant court rules say about the ability of either party to ask for a closed hearing or to invoke the *exclusionary rule.*

16.25 I want to do a great job testifying as a witness in my divorce trial. What are some tips?

Keep the following in mind to be a good witness on your own behalf:

- Tell the truth. While this may not be always be comfortable, it is critical if you want your testimony to be believed by the judge.
- Listen carefully to the complete question before thinking of your answer. Wait to consider your answer until the full question is asked.
- Slow down. It's easy to speed up our speech when we are anxious. Taking your time with your answers ensures that the judge hears you and that the court staff and video recording can accurately record your testimony.
- If you don't understand a question or don't know the answer, say so.
- If the question calls for a "yes" or "no" answer, simply say so. Then wait for the attorney to ask you the next question. If there is more you want to explain, remember that you have already told your attorney all the important facts and he or she will make sure you are allowed to give any testimony significant in your case.
- Don't argue with the judge or the lawyers.
- Take your time. You may be asked some questions that call for a thoughtful response. If you need a moment to reflect on an answer before you give it, allow yourself that time.

- Stop speaking if an objection is made by one of the lawyers. Wait until the judge has decided whether to allow you to answer.

16.26 Should I be worried about being cross-examined by my spouse's lawyer at trial?

If your case goes to trial, prepare to be asked some questions by your spouse's lawyer. Many of these questions will call for a simple "yes" or "no." Other questions may, or may not, be difficult.

If you are worried about particular questions, discuss your concerns with your attorney. He or she can support you in giving a truthful response. Focus on preparing well for being asked questions by your spouse's lawyer. Try not to take the questions personally; realize that the lawyer is fulfilling a duty to advocate for your spouse's interests. Remember that you are just doing your best to tell the truth about the facts.

16.27 What happens on the day of trial?

Although no two trials are alike, the following steps will occur in most divorce trials:

- Attorneys give opening statements.
- Plaintiff's attorney calls plaintiff's witnesses to testify. Defendant's attorney may cross-examine each of them.
- Defendant's attorney calls defendant's witness to testify. Plaintiff's attorney may cross-examine each of them.
- Plaintiff's lawyer calls any rebuttal witnesses, that is, witnesses whose testimony contradicts the testimony of the defendant's witnesses.
- Closing arguments are made first by the plaintiff's attorney and then by the defendant's attorney.

16.28 Will the judge decide my case the day I go to court?

Possibly. Often, there is so much information from the trial for the judge to consider that it is not possible for the judge to give an immediate ruling.

The judge may want to review documents, review the law, perform calculations, review his or her notes, and give thoughtful consideration to the issues to be decided. Sometimes, the judge requests that counsel submit further briefing or documents after the trial is over. For this reason, it may be days, weeks, or in some cases even longer before a ruling is made.

When a judge does not make a ruling immediately upon the conclusion of a trial, it is said that the case has been "taken under advisement."

17

Appeals

You may find that, despite your best efforts to settle your case, your divorce went to trial and the judge made major decisions that will have a serious impact on your future that you believe were wrong. You may be gravely disappointed or even shocked by the judge's ruling.

The judge might have seen your case differently than you and your attorney did. Perhaps the judge made mistakes. Or it may be that Nevada law simply does not allow for the outcome you were hoping for.

Whatever the reasons for the court's rulings, you may feel that the judge's decisions are not ones that you can live with. If this is the case, talk to your lawyer immediately about your right to appeal. Together you can decide whether an appeal is in your best interests, or whether it is better to accept the court's ruling and invest your energy in moving forward without an appeal. As with everything through the divorce process, start small.

17.1 How much time after my divorce do I have to file an appeal?

You must file an appeal within thirty days after notice of the final order you wish to appeal. Because your attorney may also recommend filing certain motions following your trial, discuss your appeal rights with your lawyer as soon as you have received the judge's ruling. For some additional explanation of how the appeal process works in Nevada, and the deadlines involved, see http://willicklawgroup.com/appeals/.

A timely discussion with your attorney about your right to appeal is essential so important deadlines are not missed.

17.2 Can I appeal a temporary order?

No. Under Nevada law, usually only final orders may be appealed.

17. 3 What parts of the decree can be appealed?

If you or your spouse is unhappy with final decisions made by the judge in your case, either of you can file an appeal. Decisions that can be appealed include custody, parenting time, child support, alimony, property division, and attorney's fees.

17. 4 Will my attorney recommend I appeal specific aspects of the decree, or will I have to request it?

Your attorney may counsel you to file an appeal on certain issues of your case; you may also ask your lawyer whether there is a legitimate basis for an appeal of any decision you believe is wrong. Talk to your attorney regarding the decisions that are most unsatisfactory to you.

Your lawyer may be able to advise which issues have the greatest likelihood of success on appeal, in light of the facts of your case and Nevada law. If your divorce lawyer is not well experienced in litigating appeals, ask for a referral to experienced appellate counsel.

17.5 When should an appeal be filed?

An appeal should be filed only after careful consultation with your lawyer when you believe that the judge has made a serious error under the law or the facts of your case. Among the factors you and your attorney should discuss are:

- Whether the judge had the authority under the law to make the decisions set forth in your decree
- The likelihood of the success of your appeal
- The risk that an appeal by you will encourage an appeal by your former spouse
- The cost of the appeal

- The length of time an appeal can be expected to take
- The impact of a delay in the case during the appeal

The deadline for filing an appeal is thirty days from the date that a final order is entered in your case. It is important that you are clear about the deadline that applies in your case, so talk to your attorney at once if you are thinking about an appeal.

17.6 Are there any disadvantages to filing an appeal?

There can be disadvantages to filing an appeal, including:

- Uncertainty as to the outcome
- Increased attorney's fees and costs
- The risk of a worse outcome on appeal than you received at trial
- Delay in finalizing your divorce
- Prolonged conflict between you and your former spouse
- Risk of a second trial occurring after the appeal
- Difficulty in obtaining closure and moving forward with your life

17.7 How do I decide whether to appeal?

An appeal is *not* a retrial of the action. As to discretionary matters, the judge might have simply seen the equities differently than did the client and counsel. It may be that Nevada law simply did not allow for the desired outcome. Or, perhaps, the judge made mistakes.

All three of those possibilities provide the possibility for an altered resolution on appeal, but the relative chances—and difficulty—of achieving an altered result are vastly different among the three, so accurately perceiving what happened at trial and why is critical.

The "common wisdom" is that only about 10 to 20 percent of civil cases are reversed on appeal. While these statistics are still not wildly encouraging, "one in four" is a lot better than "one in ten." Still, the best odds of a favorable outcome on appeal are gained from accurately assessing the chance of prevailing on appeal before filing.

While not every appeal concerns economic issues, just about every appeal has economic consequences. A critical issue to consider as to a possible appeal is its estimated cost versus the financial benefit of prevailing. For financial cases, that can usually be at least projected. For non-financial cases, such as custody or relocation, this basically requires putting a price tag on the decision involved.

Then there is the "cost" in time in continued legal actions, since an appeal usually takes a year or more, and often double that. While it could conceivably be faster, no such guarantee can be given, and there is an emotional cost to not being able to reach finality—good or bad—and moving on with your life.

There is the reality that there is a measure of unpredictability: a bad decision on appeal is possible no matter the perceived merits of the case.

In short, the decision as to whether or not to appeal should take into consideration the possible outcomes, the cost of litigation, and the emotional investment.

17.8 Are the services of an attorney necessary to appeal?

Probably. The appeals process is very detailed and specific, with set deadlines and specific court rules.

It is *possible* for a proper person litigant to file and prosecute an appeal. Nevada does have a program permitting proper person appeals. However, few people without legal training are able to put together a convincing appellate case. While it is likely that some such litigants have been successful, none of the cases in the recent family law list of significant decisions appear to have been prosecuted by a proper person litigant.

Given the complex nature of the appellate process, you should have an attorney if you intend to file an appeal.

17.9 Should I have the same lawyer who handled my divorce do the appeal?

Probably not, unless your divorce lawyer is also familiar with appeals. The reality is that the appeals process has rules and procedures very different from those governing trial practice. Even a gifted trial lawyer requires use of a different skill set to evaluate, write, and speak as an effective appellate advocate, and there is a learning curve to acquiring those skills.

Everything on appeal is different than in trial court. The written submissions on appeal are not merely recycled trial court briefs and motions. Generally, a brief written by an experienced appellate attorney is a very different product than one coming from trial counsel.

There is also the emotional component to consider. Trial counsel are sometimes as emotionally invested in their cases as their clients are, and lack the objectivity necessary to really see the merits of a case on appeal. An appellate attorney is trained to look at the result, and the record, cold—the same way the Nevada Supreme Court will see it.

The reality is that trial counsel may not be best suited to handle a case once it enters the world of appeals. It is often in the client's best interest to obtain separate appellate counsel.

17.10 How long does the appeals process usually take?

It depends. An appeal can take anywhere from several months to well over a year. An appeal may also result in the appellate court requiring further proceedings by the trial court (this is called *remand*). This will result in further delay.

17.11 What are the steps in the appeals process?

There are many steps which your lawyer will take on your behalf in the appeal process, including:

- Identifying the issues to be appealed
- Filing a notice with the court of your intent to appeal
- Attending an appellate settlement conference—the last opportunity, usually, to try to settle an appeal before fully litigating it
- Obtaining the necessary court documents and trial exhibits to send to the appellate court
- Obtaining a transcript of trial, a written copy of testimony by witnesses and statements by the judge and the lawyers made in the presence of the court reporter (or transcript of recording)
- Performing legal research to support your arguments on appeal

- Preparing and filing a document known as a *brief,* which sets forth the facts of the case and relevant law, complete with citations to the court transcript, court documents, and prior cases
- Making an oral argument before the judges of the appellate court
- Waiting for a decision, which could take days, but much more often takes many weeks or months after argument, for a decision by the appellate court

17.12 Is filing and pursuing an appeal expensive?

Yes. In addition to filing fees and lawyer fees, there is likely to be a substantial cost for the preparation of the transcript of the trial testimony and other documents.

17.13 If I do not file an appeal, can I ever go back to court to change my decree?

Certain aspects of a decree are normally not modifiable, such as the division of property and debts or an award of attorney fees. Other parts of your decree, such as support or matters regarding the children, may be modified if there has been a "material and substantial change in circumstances."

A modification of custody or parenting time for minor children will also require you to show that the change would be in their best interest.

If your decree did not provide for alimony or if it ordered that the alimony be non-modifiable, it is unlikely that you will have any basis for a modification. If you believe that you have a basis for a modification of your divorce decree, consult with your attorney.

In Closing

Take a moment to acknowledge yourself. While you may see that you have not always been your finest self during the divorce, no doubt you have done your best to make it through each day. You are looking anew at your relationships, the needs of your children, your financial security, and yourself. You are demonstrating tremendous courage.

Consider how many invaluable lessons you have learned during your marriage and during your divorce. Then spend some time envisioning a brighter future, knowing that, often our expectations really do direct our reality. Looking forward rather than behind will give you hope and energy for taking the next small step beyond divorce and toward your future.

As each day takes you closer to the completion of your divorce, you move nearer to your new life—a fresh start and endless possibilities. All the best to you on your journey.

Resources

Family Courts

First Judicial District Court (no separate Family Court)
855 East Musser Street, Suite 3031
Carson City, Nevada 89701
E-mail: districtcourtclerk@carson.org
www.carson.org

Second Judicial District Court
Family Division
One South Sierra Street, 3rd Floor
Reno, Nevada 89501
www.washoecourts.com

Fourth Judicial District Court (no separate Family Court)
571 Idaho Street
Elko, Nevada 89801
www.elkocountynv.net

Fifth Judicial District Court (no separate Family Court)
Department 1:
Post Office Box 393
Tonopah, NV 89049
Phone: (775) 482-8141
Department 2:
1520 E. Basin Avenue, Suite 105
Pahrump, NV 89060
Phone: (775) 945-2446
www.nyecounty.net

Sixth Judicial District Court (no separate Family Court)
Serving Humboldt, Lander, and Pershing Counties
http://sixthjudicialdistrict.com

Seventh Judicial District Court (no separate Family Court)
Serving Eureka, Lincoln, and White Pine Counties
www.lincolncountynv.org/courts.htm

Eighth Judicial District Court
Family Courts and Service Center
601 North Pecos Road
Las Vegas, Nevada 89101
www.clarkcountycourts.us/ejdc/

Eighth Judicial District Court
Family Division
Regional Justice Center
200 Lewis Avenue
Las Vegas, Nevada 89155
www.clarkcountycourts.us/ejdc/

Family Resources

Child Protective Services
Phone: (702) 455-8700

Child Haven
701 North Pecos Road
Las Vegas, Nevada 89101
Phone: (702) 455-5390

Court Appointed Special Advocate (CASA)
601 North Pecos Drive
Las Vegas, Nevada 89101
Phone: (702) 455-5297
FAX: (702) 455-4306
E-mail: parkss@clarkcountycourts.us

Drug Court Program
Phone: (702) 671-4593

Family Youth Services
Phone: (702) 455-5210

Family Mediation Center
601 North Pecos Road, Suite ADG-450
Las Vegas, Nevada 89101
Phone: (702) 455-2158
FAX: (702) 455-4186

Family Violence Intervention Program
Phone: (702) 455-0027
FAX: (702) 455-3400

Fiscal Services
Phone: (702) 671-4593

Interpretive Services
Phone: (702) 671-4578 (RJC)
Phone: (702) 455-1878 **(Family Courts - 601 Pecos)**

Master Calendar
Phone: (702) 455-5309
FAX: (702) 384-3067

Mental Health Program
Phone: (702) 671-3319

Probate Commissioner (601 Pecos)
Phone: (702) 455-2650
FAX: 455-5551

Self-Help Center for Family Court
Phone: (702) 455-1500
FAX: (702) 382-1090

Transcript/Video Service (Family Court)
Phone: (702) 455-4977

Ninth Judicial District Court (no separate Family Court)
Douglas County

E-filing assistance for Family Court:
Clark County
Wiznet Help Desk
Phone: (702) 671-0514
Tyler Technologies
E-mail: efiling.support@tylertech.com

Washoe County
Tech Support
Phone: (775) 328-3518
E-mail: Courttech@washoecourts.us

Supreme Court

Nevada Supreme Court
201 South Carson, Suite 300
Carson City, Nevada 89701
Phone: (800) 992-0900
E-mail: nvscclerk@nvcourts.nv.gov
and
200 Lewis Avenue, 17th Floor
Las Vegas, Nevada 89101

Federal Courts

United States District Court
District of Nevada
Lloyd George Building
333 Las Vegas Boulevard, South
Las Vegas, Nevada 89101

United States Bankruptcy Court
District of Nevada
Foley Federal Building, 4th Floor
300 Las Vegas Boulevard South
Las Vegas, Nevada 89101
and
United States Bankruptcy Court
District of Nevada
300 Booth Street, Room 1109
Reno, Nevada 89509
(775) 784-5559

Court of Appeals (9th Circuit)
333 Las Vegas Boulevard, South, Room 7072
Las Vegas, Nevada 89101

State Bar

State Bar of Nevada
600 East Charleston Boulevard
Las Vegas, NV 89104
www.nvbar.org

Pro Bono Assistance

Legal Aid Center of Southern Nevada
800 South Eighth Street
Las Vegas, Nevada 89101
Phone: (702) 386-1070
FAX: (702) 386-1796 www.lacsn.org

Legal Aid Center of Southern Nevada was established in 1958, and is a private, non-profit, 501(c) (3) organization that ensures equal access to justice through free legal advice and representation for those who cannot afford to hire an attorney. Service areas include domestic violence, child abuse, consumer fraud, and Social Security. Free classes are offered in bankruptcy, divorce, custody, small claims, guardianship, and foreclosure. Funding is provided through private donations, government grants, and *pro bono* hours donated by local attorneys.

Child Support Assistance

District Attorney's Office
Child Support Division
Phone: (702) 455-4755

Clark County District Attorney
Family Support Division
1900 East Flamingo Road, Suite 100
Las Vegas, NV 89119
Phone: (702) 671-9200
FAX:(702) 366-2400

Other Family Related Services

Willick Law Group
Online website and library
http://willicklawgroup.com/

Clark County Family Law Self-Help Center
Family Courts and Services Center
601 North Pecos
Las Vegas, NV 89155
Hours of Service
Monday—Friday 8:00 A.M. to 4:00 P.M.
http://www.clarkcountycourts.us/shc/

Washoe County Family Law Self-Help Center
One South Sierra, 1st Floor
Reno, NV 89501
Phone: (775) 325-6731
Hours of Operation
Monday—Thursday 8:30-4:30 P.M.
www.washoecourts.com/index.cfm?page-selfhelp

Public Employees' Retirement System of Nevada (PERS)
693 West Nye Lane
Carson City, Nevada 89703
Phone: (775) 687-5131

Domestic Violence Assistance:

National Domestic Violence Hotline
Phone: (800) 799-7233

Nevada Network Against Domestic Violence
220 South Rock Boulevard, Suite 7,
Reno, NV 89502
Phone: (775) 828-1115 or (800) 500-1556 (In State)
FAX: (775) 828-9911
www.nnadv.org

Family Violence Intervention Program
Phone: (702) 455-0027
FAX: (702) 455-3400

Safe Nest
Phone: (702) 646-4981 (or rural at (800) 486-7282)

Safe House
Phone: (702) 564-3227

United Way of Northern Nevada and the Sierra
Phone: 775-333-8287

American Academy of Matrimonial Lawyers (AAML)
aaml.org

Center for Divorce Education & Online Coparent Education
Phone: (877) 874-1365
E-mail: info@divorce-education.com

Find-a-Lawyer Resources

AAML
http://aaml.org/find-a-lawyer

Martindale.com
www.martindale.com/Find-Lawyers-and-Law-Firms.aspx

Lawyers.com
http://www.lawyers.com/

AVVO
http://www.avvo.com/find-a-lawyer

Divorce Center
7472 West Sahara Avenue, Suite 102-C
Las Vegas, Nevada 89117
Phone: (702) 735-7200
FAX (702) 735-8191
E-mail: divorcecenter@aol.com

Equal Rights for Divorced Fathers
23 North Mojave Road, Suite A
Las Vegas, Nevada 89101
Phone: (702) 387-6266
www.EqualRightsForFathers.com

Family Solutions, Inc.
8440 West Lake Mead Boulevard, Suite 206
Las Vegas, Nevada 89128
Phone (702) 395-8417
FAX: (702) 242-4429

Women's Divorce Clinic
3907 Kohler Way
North Las Vegas, Nevada 89032
Phone: (702) 368-3531
FAX: (702) 368-3532
E-mail: klowe@legal-self-help.com

Glossary

16.2 Disclosures: The materials, information, and documents required by the court rules to be turned over to the other party very early on in the case (and supplemented as the case proceeds), even if the other party does not request them.

A

Affidavit: A written statement of facts made under oath and signed before a notary public. Affidavits are usually made by a party, or by a witness to some fact or event. The person signing the affidavit may be referred to as the *affiant*. Affidavits may be used instead of live testimony in open court, or in court filings prior to such hearings. Normally, the attorney prepares the affidavit from information supplied by whoever is to sign it.

Alimony: Sometimes called *spousal support* or *maintenance*. Court-ordered payments from one party to another, in periodic payments or a lump sum, that are neither property division payments nor child support payments.

Allegation: A statement that one party claims is true.

Answer: A written response to the complaint for divorce. It serves to admit or deny the allegations in the complaint and may also make claims against the opposing party. This is sometimes called a *responsive pleading*. Unless the time is extended, an answer is normally due within twenty days of service of a complaint on the defendant.

Appeal: The process by which a higher court reviews the decision of a lower court. In Nevada family law cases, all appeals are made to the Nevada Supreme Court, although at this writing there is a proposal pending that could create a Court of Appeals to which many family law cases could be diverted for resolution.

C

Case management conference (CMC): A procedural meeting, with the judge, both attorneys, and both parties, to determine how the case will proceed, how long before a trial can be set, and some other matters.

Child support: Financial support for a child paid by the noncustodial parent to the custodial parent, or from one joint physical custodian to the other if there is a variance between the parties' incomes.

Closed hearing: The right of a party to exclude from the courtroom everyone except court staff, the parties, their lawyers, and certain other persons.

Community property: Generally, property acquired by the husband or wife, or both, during the marriage, and subject to division upon divorce.

Complaint: The first document filed with the court in an action for divorce, separate maintenance, annulment, or paternity. The complaint sets forth the facts on which the requested relief is based.

Contempt of court: The willful and intentional failure of a party to comply with a court order, judgment, or decree. Contempt, if found, may be punishable by a fine or jail.

Contested case: Any case in which the parties cannot reach an agreement. A contested case, if not settled, results in a trial to have the judge decide disputed issues.

Court order: A court-issued document setting forth the judge's orders. An order can be issued based upon the parties' agreement or the judge's decision. An order may require the parties to perform certain acts or set forth their rights and responsibilities. An order is put in writing, signed by the judge, and filed with the court.

Court Order Acceptable for Processing (COAP): A type of court order that provides for payment of federal civil service retirement benefits to a former spouse.

Cross-examination: The questioning of a witness by the opposing counsel during a trial, evidentiary hearing, or at a deposition, in response to questions asked by the other lawyer.

Civil Service Retirement System (CSRS): The federal retirement system in place before 1984.

Custody: As applied to children it means the physical possession of a child, or the legal right and responsibility to make decisions relating to a child, or both. *See legal custody* and *physical custody.*

D

Decree of divorce: A final court order dissolving the marriage. Usually, the same document divides property and debts, orders support, and enters other orders regarding finances and the custody and support of minor children.

Defendant: The responding party to a divorce; the party who did not file the complaint initiating the divorce.

Deposition: A witness's testimony taken out of court, under oath, and in the presence of lawyers and a court reporter. If a person gives different testimony at the time of trial, he or she can be "impeached" with the deposition testimony (that is, statements made at a deposition can be used to show untruthfulness if a different answer is given at trial).

Direct examination: The initial questioning of a witness in court by the lawyer who called that witness to the stand.

Discovery: A process used by attorneys to obtain information from the opposing party for the purpose of fully assessing a case for settlement or trial, or obtaining evidence to be used. Types of discovery include subpoenas, interrogatories, requests for production of documents, and requests for admissions.

Dissolution: Sometimes used to mean "divorce." The act of terminating or dissolving a marriage.

E

EDCR: The Eighth Judicial District Court Rules (Clark County).

Equitable distribution of property: A term sometimes used in the case law, and by lawyers and judges, for the goal of courts in distributing property and debts. Nevada law requires an equal distribution of property (and probably debts) between divorcing parties unless "compelling circumstances are found for some other distribution."

Ex parte: Usually in reference to a motion, the term used to describe an appearance of only one party before the judge, without the other party being present, and sometimes without advance notice to the other party of the request made to the judge. For example, a joint preliminary injunction may be granted immediately upon the filing of a complaint for divorce.

Exclusive possession: The right of a party, usually pursuant to a temporary court order, to the possession and use of an asset, such as a home or car.

Exclusionary rule: A right that can be invoked by either party during a hearing or trial to order prospective witnesses out of the courtroom until they have concluded giving their testimony.

F

Family mediation center (FMC): The court facility at which parties may attempt to negotiate issues relating to child custody and visitation with the assistance of a neutral mediator.

Federal Employes Retirement System (FERS): The federal retirement system in place since 1984.

Financial disclosure form (FDF): The court-approved form required by both sides reporting their income, assets, and expenses, which is required with every motion, and prior to a trial. Previously, a version of this form was known as an AFC, or affidavit of financial condition.

G

Guardian *ad litem* (GAL): A person, often a lawyer or mental health professional, appointed by the court to conduct an investigation or to provide a report to the court regarding a child's best interest.

H

Hague Convention: While there are several such "conventions" (international treaties), usually the term is used in family law to refer to the treaty dealing with civil remedies for the international kidnaping of children.

Hearing: Any proceeding before the court for the purpose of resolving disputed issues through presentation of testimony, affidavits, exhibits, or argument.

Hold-harmless clause: A term in a court order that requires one party to assume responsibility for a debt and to protect the other party from any loss or expense in connection with it, as in "to hold harmless from liability" for a credit card debt.

I

Impeachment: The process of questioning the truthfulness of the testimony of a witness by presenting prior testimony from that witness, or documentary evidence, contrary to the testimony now being offered.

Interrogatories: Written questions sent from one party to the other that are used to obtain facts or opinions related to the divorce.

J

Joint custody: The shared right and responsibility of both parents for either physical possession of a child, or for legal care and decision making for a child, or for both physical and legal custody. For physical custody, a custodial time share of anywhere from 50/50 to 60/40 is considered "joint custody."

Joint preliminary injunction (JPI): An order often issued at the beginning of a case generally forbidding either party from harassing the other, removing the children permanently from Nevada, or disposing of any community or other joint property without agreement of the other party or court order.

Jurisdiction: Authority of a court to make rulings affecting a party. Also, sometimes, means the place of a court decision.

L

Legal custody: The right and responsibility to make decisions and provide care for a child, including making major decisions regarding the child, including the child's health, education, and religious upbringing.

M

Mediation: A process by which a neutral third party facilitates negotiations between the parties on some or all issues.

Motion: A written application to the court to make or change orders on issues, before trial or after a decree is issued, on any subject over which the court has jurisdiction, such as child support, custody, monetary issues, etc.

Motion for relocation: A parent's request to the court seeking permission to relocate to another state with the child or children.

Motion to modify: A party's written request to the court to change a prior order regarding custody, child support, alimony, or any other order, before or after trial, that the court may change by law.

N

No-fault divorce: Divorce entered at the request of one party to a marriage which does not require evidence or proof of "fault" or marital misconduct. This means that traditional "grounds" for divorce such as abandonment, cruelty, and adultery are irrelevant to the issue of whether a divorce will be granted in modern practice.

Notice of entry (NOE): The formal document sent to the court showing that an order has been sent to the other party. This starts various time deadlines.

NRCP: The Nevada Rules of Civil Procedure.

O

Opposition: The written response by a party to a motion filed by the other party.

P

Parenting plan: A document setting out the physical custody, and sometimes the support, of a child of the marriage. Such a document can be negotiated, mediated, or ordered by a court without agreement of the parties.

Party: The person in a legal action whose rights or interests will be affected by the divorce. For example, in a divorce the parties include the wife and husband.

Pending: A term meaning during the case, or until an order is issued. For example, the judge may award a party temporary support while the case is pending, or temporary exclusive possession of a house pending a hearing on the issue.

Petitioner: A term formerly used to refer to the plaintiff or person who files the complaint seeking a divorce.

Physical custody: The time that a child physically spends in the care of a party, including the time the child resides with the party and that party provides supervision for the child and makes the day-to-day decisions regarding the child. Usually, this time includes periods in which the child is actually physically remote from that party for school, visiting relatives, activities, etc., at the direction of the party with physical custody.

Plaintiff: The person who files the complaint initiating a divorce.

Pleadings: Technically, only the *divorce complaint, answer,* and *reply*. Sometimes used loosely to describe any documents filed with the court seeking a court order.

Q

Qualified Domestic Relations Order (QDRO): A type of court order that divides a retirement account, plan, or payment stream between parties, or provides for direct payment from a retirement account to a former spouse or certain other eligible payees. Sometimes used loosely to refer to any retirement plan division order, including those through the military, the Civil Service, or Nevada PERS.

Qualified Medical Child Support Order (QMCSO): A type of court order that provides medical benefits for a minor child and provides to a former spouse certain rights regarding medical insurance and information.

R

Reply: The formal written response by a plaintiff to the answer filed by a defendant. Also used to refer to any rebuttal document filed by a moving party to respond to the opposing filing filed by the other party.

Request for admissions: A written request for the other party to admit or deny allegations relevant to the case sent from one party to the other during the discovery process.

Request for production of documents: A written request for documents sent from one party to the other during the discovery process.

S

Separate property: Generally, property acquired by either the husband or wife before marriage, and property acquired during marriage by gift, bequest, devise, descent, or award for personal injury damages, with the rents, issues, and profits thereof. In divorce cases, usually used to refer to property that is not community property, and is not to be divided during the divorce.

Service: The process of notifying a party about a legal filing. "Proof of service" is the document establishing that such notice was given.

Setoff: A debt or financial obligation owed by one spouse that is deducted from the debt or financial obligation owed by the other spouse.

Settlement: The agreed resolution of disputed issues.

Show cause: The process by which a party is required to prove that he or she is not in contempt of court for violating or failing to comply with a court order. Usually, the process is begun by a motion for an "order to show cause," requiring the holding of such a hearing.

Stipulation: An agreement reached between parties or their attorneys.

Subpoena: A document delivered to a person or witness that requires him or her to appear in court, appear for a deposition, or produce documents. Failure to comply could result in punishment by the court. A subpoena requesting documents is called a subpoena *duces tecum*.

T

Temporary orders: Usually, orders entered during a divorce case as to any issue that remain effective until changed or until a final decree is issued.

Temporary Protective Order (TPO): An order, usually made by a hearing master and approved by the court, making short-term orders to stay away from the party obtaining the order. It may also provide for custody, possession of a home, or some other matters, and sometimes is issued without notice to the other party. When issued *ex parte,* such an order is usually followed shortly by a hearing at which both parties can appear and argue the merits of extending or terminating such an order.

Temporary Restraining Order (TRO): An order of the court prohibiting a party from certain behavior. For example, a temporary restraining order may order a person not to transfer any funds during a pending divorce action.

Trial: A formal court hearing usually involving the introduction of testimony and documentary evidence, and argument in which the judge decides disputed issues.

U

Uniform Child Custody Jurisdiction and Enforcement Act (UCCJEA): The law effective in almost every state that determines which court can make an order regarding child custody.

Uniform Interstate Family Support Act (UIFSA): The law effective in every state that determines which court can make an order regarding child and spousal support.

Under advisement: A term used to describe the status of a ruling or decision in a case, usually after a court hearing on a motion or a trial, when the judge has not yet made a decision.

W

WDCR: The Washoe County District Court Rules.

Index

About the Author

Marshal S. Willick is the principal of the Willick Law Group, an A/V rated family law firm in Las Vegas, Nevada, where he practices trial and appellate family law. He is a certified family law specialist, a fellow of both the American and International Academies of Matrimonial Lawyers (AAML and IAML), former chair of the Nevada Bar Family Law Section, and former president of the Nevada chapter of the AAML. He has authored many books and articles on family law and retirement benefits issues; he was also managing editor of the *Nevada Family Law Practice Manual*. He is frequently a teacher of continuing legal education classes and is often sought as a lecturer on family law issues.

In addition to litigating trial and appellate cases in Nevada, Willick has participated in hundreds of divorce and pension cases in the trial and appellate courts of other states; he has also participated in the drafting of various state and federal statutes in the areas of divorce and property division. Willick has chaired many committees of the American Bar Association Family Law Section, AAML, and Nevada Bar; has served on many more committees, boards, and commissions of those organizations; and has been called on to represent the entire ABA in Congressional hearings on military pension matters. He has served as an alternate judge in various courts, and frequently testifies as an expert witness. He serves on the board of directors for the Legal Aid Center of Southern Nevada.

Willick received his bachelor of arts degree, with honors, from the University of Nevada at Las Vegas in 1979, and his juris doctor from Georgetown University Law Center in Washington, D.C., in 1982. Before entering private practice, he served on the central legal staff of the Nevada Supreme Court for two years.

Willick can be reached by e-mail at Marshal@willicklawgroup.com, and additional information is available from the Willick firm websites, www.willicklawgroup.com and www.qdromasters.com.

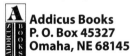